TERRORISM:
WHY AMERICA IS THE TARGET

By
Dr. Mohammad T. Mehdi

New World Press
230 E. 44 Street, #3F
New York, NY 10017

Library of Congress Catalog Card No. 87-62974

ISBN # 0-911119-10-8

Printed in the United States of America

Table of Contents

Other books by the author

CONSTITUTIONALISM:
WESTERN AND MIDDLE EASTERN (1960)

A NATION OF LIONS . . . CHAINED (1962)

PEACE IN THE MIDDLE EAST (1967)

GENERAL THEORY OF LAW AND STATE
By Hans Kelsen (Translated into Arabic)

KENNEDY AND SIRHAN . . . WHY? (1968)

PALESTINE AND THE BIBLE (1970)
(Edited)

PEACE IN PALESTINE (1976)

Dedication

To the victims of war and terrorism.

Preface

There is a new crisis on the international scene, difficult to define, locate and remedy. It is the problem of terrorism which defies the traditional ways of combating as in acts of wars and other forms of violence.

And unhappily, America is the target of terrorism!

With all its might and intelligence gathering ability, the "terrorists" have continued, and undoubtedly will continue, their attacks on America. Why and what is the cause? The answer to these questions is essential first step in the process of providing the remedy!

This book deals with the question of terrorism and attempts to define it and suggests the remedy to stop and eliminate this new form of violence. The hope is that it will present a challenge to the readers to think in new terms. If it erks and irritates some readers, that will be a tribute to the thinking process in the open society. If that happens, the author will feel rewarded.

The manuscript was typed by Barbara Hart (and her fetus) to whom I am grateful. How was she able to read my bad handwriting and transcribe my dictation is beyond me! I am also grateful to my daughters Anisa, Janan and Laila and momie Beverlee who have one way or another contributed to the making of this book. My friends Ghazi Khankan, Ellen Weber, Bob Schutz, Ayyoub Talhami and my brother Dr. M. R. have all been helpful with their ideas, suggestions and arguments.

The book is dedicated to the victims of war and terrorism. Let's hope that it will help eliminate both those evils.

MTM

New York City
December 15, 1987

Introduction

On April 15, 1986 at 2:00 A.M. (Central European Time), (April 14 at 7:00 P.M. (EST), the mighty United States of America attacked a tenth rate military power, the Libyan Arab Jamahiryyah, some 5,000 miles away on the coast of North Africa.

Within hours, worldwide demonstrations erupted against America. Governments in Western Europe, the Middle East, Asia, and Africa denounced the U.S. action as a case of naked aggression. Attacks on American embassies and consulates as well as on individual Americans increased immediately.

These protests were the reaction of three-fourths of the people and governments of the world against the U.S. bombing of Tripoli and Benghazi. The American attack led to the death of some 100 persons, including Colonel Qaddafi's 15 month-old daughter, Hana. Civilian centers and homes, including the French Embassy, were destroyed.

The Americans were astonished that there should be such anti-American reaction and universal disapproval of U.S. policies. Haven't the Americans been contributing billions of dollars in foreign aid? And wasn't the U.S. attack a reaction against terrorism which had been sponsored by Qaddafi?

On radio and television talk shows, former CIA and State Department officials, who were failures then as officials, appeared as "experts on the Middle East." They told the Americans, "We are good; they are evil" stories and "We are right; they are wrong" tales. "They" are the terrorists and Communists; "we" are the people opposed to terrorism and all other forms of evil!

And what is terrorism? Terrorism is a violent act against civilians for a political goal of which we disapprove. If we approve of the political goal, then the violence will be the action of freedom fighters!

The U.S. government defines "terrorism" as the "unlawful use of force or violence against persons or property to intimidate or coerce a government, the civilian population, or any segment thereof, in furtherance of political or social objectives." And a "terrorist incident in America is a violent act or an act dangerous to human life in

1

violation of the criminal laws of the United States or of any state to intimidate or coerce a government, the civilian population, or any segment thereof, in furtherance of political or social objectives."

The FBI reports that in 1985 in the United States there were seven terrorist incidents, resulting in two killed and ten injured. Two incidents were carried out by "volunteers for the Puerto Rican Revolution;" one by "Red Guerrilla Resistance," and four incidents by "Jewish extremist elements."[1]

On the international level in 1985, there were 12 Americans killed out of more than 250 killed and injured in terrorist attacks.

But why the attacks on Americans and the protests against America? Any why aren't there acts of terrorism against Russia or hijacking of Russian planes? The fact is that there are, indeed, hijackings of Russian planes and acts of "terrorism" directed against Russia. But these acts are not reported as dramatically in this country, as they are of little news value compared with the hijacking of the Achille Lauro or TWA Flight 847. Americans want to hear the news of Americans. The death of one American abroad is more newsworthy than the death of 1,000 Indonesians in Jakarta. Not only do most Americans not care, but many do not even know where Jakarta is!

In Afghanistan, wherein the Russians are having a war of suppression against the people of that land, the "Mujahedeen" are engaged in counter "war" or "terrorism" against Russian invaders. And the Afghani Mujahedeen have engaged in "heroic" acts against Russia which, if carried out by the Palestinians against the Israelis or their American sponsors would be considered as acts of "terrorism." Or are the Afghani Mujahedeen engaged in acts of terrorism against Russians? The Afghanis attack the Russians because the Russians have attacked them, just as the Palestinians attack the Israelis and their sponsors, the Americans, because the Israelis have occupied their land and attacked them with the military aid of the United States.

But why the attacks on innocent individual Americans who are on vacation or business of some kind? As a matter of fact, the Palestinians should fly their airplanes to Washington, D.C. and bomb the Pentagon and the State Department and Congress rather than attacking individual Americans! Happily, however, the Palestinians do not have long-range airplanes equipped for such attacks, and so they do the next bad thing: attack individual, innocent Americans!

Of course, if Americans believe that it is legitimate for the Euro-

2

pean and Zionist Jews of the U.S.A. and elsewhere to occupy the land of the Palestinians, Syrians, Lebanese and Egyptians, then the Americans should, of course, support the Israelis. However, in such a case, Americans should not cry "foul" if the Palestinians and other Arabs try to fight back and hit at the sponsors of the Zionist occupiers of Palestine.

To support Israel in killing thousands of Arabs and then to cry that the Arabs have killed a few Americans, is not fair. The Palestinians attack the Americans because the Americans are sponsors of Israel and are engaged in a proxy war against the Arabs. American violence and proxy war against the Arabs breeds violence and terrorism. The cause of Arab terrorism, therefore, has to be seen in American policy toward Palestine. Palestine is the question, not Sinai. Indeed, Zionist occupation of Palestine, with American help, is the root of the American crisis in the Middle East.

Terrorism against America is a belated reaction to American proxy wars or proxy oppression of other people. If you kill "A" or help "B" to kill "A", the supporters of "A" will try to retaliate. They will use whatever devices are at their disposal to seek revenge or otherwise redress their grievance. Americans should not be astonished nor should they complain.

In this sense, Palestinian "terrorism" is retaliation against some 40 years of proxy American war conducted against the Palestinians and the Arabs. The United States government's support of European and other Zionist groups in occupying Palestine means to the Palestinians a war carried out by America against the Palestinians.

Not that the American people or American politicians hate the Palestinians. Indeed, the American politicians do not hate the Arabs, nor do they love the Jews. But they do love themselves, of course. They want to get elected to the high offices in the land. That can be done only through elections. In order for the politician to receive at least 51 percent of the votes, he is willing to call the right, left and the left, right. Politicians have offered the moon in the process of appealing to the people. Bob Hope's observation many years ago after an election that "Now that the election is over, the alibis will begin," is more than a mere crack. It is a correct insight into the nature of American politics. And in this truism the root of most American difficulties at home and abroad may be found!

And so when we recall the horror of American Embassy hostages

3

in Iran or TWA Flight 847 or the death of an 11 year-old American girl in the Rome airport, let's ask, "Why? What is the cause?"

In his *THE AYATOLLAH IN THE CATHEDRAL*, former American hostage in the U.S. Embassy in Tehran, Moorhead Kennedy, writes that during the 444 days of captivity, he asked himself again and again,

"I know what they're doing to me.
What did we do to them?"

Chapter I

America and the World

The 250 million Americans represent four percent of the world population of five billion people. Assuming that Western Europe has another four percent of the world population, it follows that more than 85 percent of the human race live on the Afro-Asian land mass and in Latin America.

America's future will be determined in Asia, Africa and Latin America, not in Western Europe. Western Europe is the past; the other continents represent the future. Today Americans are concerned primarily with Europe. How much do they know about the future?

American politicians, the news media, and American "experts," tell the American people what *pleases* the people to hear. They do not tell the people what they should hear about the rest of the world and the attitude of the 85 percent of the human race towards America.

Americans have been told and, therefore, they "know" that they are "good" and "right," doing the proper things in the world and for the world community. If so, what is the meaning of all kinds of attacks on America and even demonstrations in Western Europe against the United States?

There are three reasons, at least, for this confusion and quandary.

1. THE HISTORIC STAGE.

The Americans think with their *hearts*, rather than their *heads*.

In the land of plenty and the rich, Americans had been isolated from the international community for about 200 years. During that period, they had nothing to do with the outside world and the refusal of the U.S. Senate to ratify the Covenant of the League of Nations in 1919 was the formal declaration of that isolationist period and mentality.

Within two decades, Americans suddenly found themselves in the "big" world, engaged in a war for freedom and democracy against the Nazis and Fascists. By 1946, the U.S. Senate ratified the Charter of the United Nations, the sign of America becoming part of the international community.

But were the American people prepared to become part of the

world community and the family of nations? They had power to dominate the world, but lacked the knowledge of the world which they claimed to be its leaders!

However, Americans' lack of knowledge of other lands was abundantly compensated for by their warmth, goodwill, charity and aid to foreign people and foreign countries. Hence, the thousands of cases of American aid to refugees, underprivileged and the disaster striken areas of the world.

This lack of knowledge, on the one hand, and expression of goodwill, on the other hand, created a confusion for many Americans when they saw that the recipients of their goodwill did not respond as they were expected. The billions of dollars America has given in foreign aid since World War II have not brought much goodwill for America in the outside world. This is confusing and often infuriating to most Americans.

The American people do, indeed, have goodwill and their rich society can afford to offer huge amounts of aid to foreign countries. But Americans do not seem to distinguish between economic aid, which as a rule is appreciated by the people of foreign lands, and military aid, which usually provides the foreign governments with tools to suppress their own people.

Furthermore, the people of America, with their goodwill, do not seem to understand that if they give economic aid to a person and then kill his brother, the recipient of the aid will object and will denounce America for the killing of his brother, despite the aid he received.

For example, if America helps one African nation and then supports the oppressors of another African nation, or helps the Arabs of Saudi Arabia and supports the Zionist Jews of Warsaw or Brooklyn to occupy the land of the Arabs of Palestine—under such circumstances all Africans and all Arabs will be against America, notwithstanding the aid given to some Africans and some Arabs.

This is common sense, but Americans have more goodwill than knowledge and so they do not see the simplest element of human behavior and reaction.

Then because of the rich society and the great material achievements in America, Americans have become, so to speak, "materialists," trying to solve all the problems of the world through material aid. In a peculiar way, Americans have adopted the economic theory of Marxism, that all problems have an economic base and are suscep-

6

tible to economic solutions. Americans, therefore, offer economic solutions to political problems.

In the Third World, the burning desire of the multitudes is the satisfaction of their emotional nationalism even more than economic aid. But the United States attempts to answer the emotional needs by offers of economic aid.

In the Middle East, the cry is for the return of the Palestinian people to their land of Palestine and the need is for American *political* help to pressure Israel to permit the Palestinians to return. The American answers, however, have come in terms of "T.V.A. on Jordan" or "Marshall Plan for the Middle East" or other economic and military aids and solutions. These are the wrong answers to what is, basically, a political question.

There is another, simplistic pattern of thinking in the American evaluation of international affairs. The United States has its international client states and offers them generous aid and support. In turn, these clients proclaim that they are "pro-American." The words "pro-America" sound like beautiful music to American ears. The "pro-America" rulers of the client states are considered to be "allies" and "good boys," deserving further American support.

In should be noted that most of these "pro-America" rulers are tyrants and dictators who oppress their own people with American financial, economic, military and political support. They receive billions of American dollars and would be stupid not to proclaim their "pro-Americanism." But the people of these countries usually hate their rulers and, likewise, hate the American sponsors of those rulers.

The United States has had the support of the Shah of Iran, Marcos of the Phillipines, Duvalier of Haiti, Sadat of Egypt, Nimeiri of the Sudan, Botha of South Africa, Pinochet of Chile, etc., while the majority of the people in those lands despised those rulers and hated America which kept them in power.

The United States politicians tell the people of America that country "x" is pro-American and then the Americans discover that the people of country "x" burn American flags and attack American establishments and embassies. At best American officials misunderstand and misread the events elsewhere. But most probably they fail, for political expediency, to inform the Americans completely and correctly as to the actual attitude of the people of those foreign countries toward America. The problem with governments is that they only deal with other governments, without taking note of the attitudes of the people ruled by those governments.

Briefly, the American people do have the goodwill. But goodwill is no substitute for knowledge, and thinking with the heart is no alternative for thinking with the head! The American people should start to think more seriously with their heads than with their hearts!

Have they been doing so? Recalling that Americans had no idea whatever of the outside world only 40 years ago, they should not be expected to become, within four short decades, authorities on North Korea, South Korea, Japan, China, Vietnam, India, south Africa, Palestine, Central America, South America, the Space Age, etc., etc., baseball, national politics and also make a living and lead a normal life!

But are they making any effort to learn about the world outside? The answer is a qualified "yes," which is gratifying. During the past 40 years, Americans have become at least 20 percent more knowledgeable about the world, thanks to the fact that America is an open society, "open" to slow, peaceful and gradual growth and change.

2. THE ACTOR.

Then there is a more immediate reason for the latest American difficulties around the world. The person of Ronald Reagan and the personality of a one-issue crusader in an age of multiple issues and general consensus. Furthermore, Mr. Reagan's Hollywood experience must be taken into consideration in the process of analyzing U.S. international policy under the Reagan Administration.

Ronald Reagan is a crusader opposed to Communism and to him, all those who disagree with American policy are either Communists or, unwittingly, supporters of Communism.

To Reagan, the world is a Hollywood set and he is the actor/director/producer. He wishes to shape the world in the image of Ronald Reagan, just as a great Hollywood director/producer creates his movies in his own image. On a Hollywood set, if "take one" is not good enough, there will be a "take two" which might be followed by "take three." And so are the efforts to shape the world community in the image of Ronald Reagan. There might have to be several "takes." If the first confrontation with Qaddafi over the Gulf of Sidra did not subjugate the Libyan leader to Reagan's will, it had to be followed by the second take, the attacks on Tripoli and Benghazi.

8

The end product must be in the image of the actor/director/ producer. The problem is that the world is not a Hollywood set and neither Ronald Reagan nor anyone else can shape it in his own image!

America is against terrorism. But terrorism has a long and deeply rooted tradition in America itself. The nation started by terrorizing the Native Americans out of their land. The lynching of the blacks was another form of terrorism, American-style. Of course, America has now been properly established and has become the defender of the *status quo*. As such, America is against change, peaceful or violent, and under the presidency of Ronald Reagan, with his "we are right; they are evil" outlook, every change is considered a violent change and an anti-American act of terrorism. Mr. Reagan uses the "national security" as the pretext to promote his anti-change philosophy. As John B. Oakes, former senior editor of *The New York Times*, put it, Reagan's "pax-Americana has more to do with ideological conformity than with national security."

Indeed, Reagan's crusade against "terrorism" has less to do with terrorism than with his anti-Communist ideology. He picks on Qaddafi of Libya and fails to pick on the terrorism of P.W. Botha of South Africa.

In his obsession with Qaddafi, Reagan issued an Executive Order on January 7, 1986 against travel to Libya, which is some 5,000 miles away, on the grounds that the North African country was "an extraordinary threat to the national security of the United States."

If Libya, with its 2.5 million population, is an "extraordinary" threat to the national security of these gigantic United States of North America, then the U.S.A. must have been established on a foundation of clay! And so was President Reagan's reasoning and attitude toward Nicaragua, considering the Sandinistas as an "extraordinary" threat to the national security of the 250 million Americans, the mightiest nation in the world. At the same time, Reagan called publicly for $100 million to aid the "contras" to carry out their terrorism against the people of Nicaragua. And at a time when the worst case of terrorism was being carried out daily in South Africa by the white, racist regime of Botha, killing tens of black people every day, Reagan was keeping the United States economic ties with Pretoria and, thereby, helping to keep the hated, racist government in power.

The Commonwealth of Nations had established a committee of

9

prominent persons to study and recommend a policy toward South Africa's *apartheid*. After months of deliberation, the committee found the government of Botha "plainly fears the adoption of effective sanctions," and that "if there are no sanctions, it will stiffen its *apartheid* policy and will resist gradual reform, thereby worsening violence in South Africa." The report maintained that "the cost in lives may have to be counted in millions." This will be "the worst bloodbath since the Second World War," it added.

At the time in which the Commonwealth committee argued that economic sanctions are the only method to avoid a South African bloodbath, the United States was arguing against economic sanctions. Secretary of State George Schultz, in a letter to Congress, maintained that sanctions would backfire by weakening the forces of moderation.

"We do not believe it should be our purpose to harm the South African economy, nor do we believe that such action will hasten the end of *apartheid*," Schultz said.

The State Department claimed that progress was being made in South Africa and neither South Africans nor Americas who are hoping to bring about peaceful change "want to destroy the South African economy."[2] But the killing, oppression and terrorism in South Africa was of no concern to the Reagan Administration; only the South African economy was of concern.

It is not terrorism that Reagan is against; it is the "terrorism" with which he disagrees that he opposes. Reagan supports "good" terrorists (such as the "contras") and is opposed to "bad" terrorists (such as the P.L.O. of the Palestinians and the African National Congress in South Africa.) The Palestinians wish to return home and the black Africans wish to attain democratic majority rule in their own country. Reagan is opposed to these goals and, hence, he is opposed to the movements.

The "good" terrorists have received more support from Reagan than the "bad" terrorists have ever received from Qaddafi.

* * *

Because the actor/producer/director wishes to create the world in his own image, Ronald Reagan will write and re-write the script, not in accordance with the facts, but rather according to his wishes and designs to shape the world.

Ronald Reagan has been obsessed with Moammar Qaddafi, and

10

Reagan has a strong desire to remove the Libyan leader from the scene. A big cowboy with power cannot tolerate a small cowboy with a big mouth! To satisfy his obsession, Reagan started with campaigns of various intensity against Qaddafi. Early in 1981, The New York Times published, what must have been a White House planted story, that Libyan terrorists were planning to assassinate the U. S. Ambassador to Italy. In a dramatic move, Ambassador Maxwell was flown out of Rome to Washington to stress the validity of the story. Later the story of the five Libyan "hit-squad" who had entered the United States, without anyone being able to discover them, to shoot Air F'orce I received front page coverage for weeks. The story also must have been planted by the Reagan Administration, as no one ever saw the "Libyan terrorists," nor was any evidence presented to the news media to prove that they existed. The American news media gobbled up the hoax, and to its discredit and shame it did not ask the Reagan Administration to present any evidence to support the claim.

The stories regarding Qaddafi's support of terrorism continued, leading to the Reagan attacks on the Gulf of Sidra and on the cities of Tripoli and Benghazi. But those attacks did not do away with Qaddafi and the Libyan leader's existence was in itself a challenge to Reagan. And so there were more Reagan planted-rumors against Qaddafi that the Libyan was disoriented and deranged. Ted Koppel stated on Nightline that "Qaddafi was known to contradict himself" after Qaddafi had made the logical statement, "We are against violence, but if the United States attacks us, we shall fight against the United States."

On August 25, 1986, the Wall Street Journal published a leading article that "The U. S. and Libya are on collision course again." The story raised some questions in the media and the Administration spokesmen said different things to different reporters. As related by The New York Times, Administration official said that The Journal's story was "a misguided, unauthorized and premature effort on the part of some people in the Administration to stimulate anti-Libyan feelings."[3]

The full story of Reagan's efforts at deceiving the news media and the American people was broken finally by Bob Woodward. The story of the planted stories was revealed in a front page article, "Qaddafi Target of Secret U. S. Deception Plan."[4] Woodward revealed that the Reagan Administration had approved a memo to launch a secret campaign of deception designed to convince

Moammar Qaddafi that he was about to be attacked again by U.S. bombers and perhaps be ousted in a *coup*.

One of the key elements of the secret strategy was to "combine real and illusionary events—through a disinformation program—with the basic goal of making Qaddafi *think* that there is a high degree of internal opposition to him within Libya, that his key trusted aides are disloyal, that the U. S. is about to move against him militarily." The story in The Wall Street Journal of August 25th, suggesting that Qaddafi was planning new acts of terrorism was to create anti-Libyan feelings in America. This was an abuse of the press and an effort to mislead American public opinion by the Administration. Thanks to Bob Woodward, who several years earlier broke the Watergate story, the news media stood up on its feet this time and defended its integrity and independence.

The U.S. Government was telling lies and deceiving the American people, supposedly to mislead the head of a foreign government. Would such lies really make a Qaddafi believe that his people were against him? The mere thinking by the Reagan Administration that Qaddafi would believe in the lies is evidence that Mr. Reagan had come to believe in his own rhetoric and misconceptions of the Libyan strongman. To say that Qaddafi is "flaky" is one thing, but to believe in the hyperbole is another. The actor/director/producer became the victim of his own imagination and efforts to shape the world in his own image, to the detriment of America and world peace!

3. THE PLAYWRIGHT.

If the media is the message, then it follows that the mind of the American people is made up to a great extent by what the news media has done or has failed to do in its reportings and in its editorials.

Thanks to *Near vs. Minnesota* 283 U.S. 697 (1931), there is no prior restraint on the printed press by governmental authorities in America. Rather, there is another form of restraint, possibly an uglier form, the so-called "self-censorship."

This "self-censorship" becomes "news management." Regretfully, most news organizations, including The New York Times, Washington Post, Los Angeles Times, CBS, NBC, ABC, etc. are guilty of the crime of news management.

For example, the American people know that Arab terrorists had attacked Rome, Vienna and Athens airports and killed six U.S. citizens. The media has reported these stories tens of times. But Americans do not know how many Palestinians, Lebanese, Syrians, Egyptians, Libyans and other Arabs have been killed by American bombs, tanks and airplanes which were given to Israel. America, in the eyes of the Arab victims, is responsible for most of the death and destruction in the Palestine area during the last three or four decades.

The fact that Americans know about the death of Leon Klinghoffer, who was killed by Palestinian terrorists, and know nothing about the murder of Alex Odeh, an American Palestinian who was most likely killed by Zionist terrorists on American soil, in Santa Ana, California, is due to the failure of the news media to inform the people about the murder of the American Palestinian while reporting at length the death of the American Jews, Leon Klinghoffer.

For many months, starting in October 1985, the American news media headlined the tragedy of the Italian liner, Achille Lauro. They damned terrorism, Palestinian terrorism and the P.L.O. They denounced Yassir Arafat, Muammar Qaddafi and, tearfully, they reported about the death of Leon Klinghoffer. The President of the United States paid a visit to Mrs. Leon Klinghoffer, after having sent her messages of condolence and talked to her on the telephone. *Ipso facto*, the press denounced the Arabs as terrorists and pronounced them guilty even before the trial.

Finally, on June 10, 1986, a report by the Italian prosecutor threw some light on the tragedy and presented a balanced evaluation. It accused the Palestinian leader, Mohammad Abbas, of masterminding the hijacking of the Italian boat. But the report defended the Palestinian cause and repeatedly praised Yassir Arafat, the chairman of the Palestinian Liberation Organization.

After the United States had skyjacked an Egyptian plane and forced it to land in Sicily, the Italian authorities released Mohammad Abbas because he held a diplomatic passport. The United States was most unhappy, as it had claimed that Abbas was the head terrorist. The Italian report said that the information provided by the United States was "inadequate" at the time, even though eventually it proved to be correct.

But the most important feature of the Italian report was a sympathetic attitude expressed toward the Palestinian movement and the right of the Palestinians to their land. It stated "this case falls within the struggle of the Palestinian people." The Palestinians, "having lost their own land, intend to carry out a struggle to reconquer their national territory and end the disastrous and inhuman effects of the new Diaspora," the report said. That loss of the land by the Palestinians is the cause of Palestinian terrorism, it must be added.

Furthermore, the report distinguished between the policies of Yassir Arafat and those of Mr. Abbas. Arafat is concerned with the military struggle inside Palestine, whereas Abbas feels that the whole world is a stage for the Palestinian struggle.[5]

Of course, there is a great deal of difference between Arafat and his policy today, and Abbas and Abu Nidal. Arafat still has some faith and hope that the political process in the West may bring some justice to his people, enabling them, ultimately, to return peacefully to their land. On the other hand, Abu Nidal and Abbas have lost all confidence in the Western sense of justice or that the political process in the West could be a device to bring justice to the Palestinians. Having lost confidence in the political process of the West, they find no alternative but to consider all the people of the Western democracies responsible for their plight. They consider it legitimate, therefore, to resort to force to return to their land. Fighting against Americans and other supporters of Israel anywhere and in whatever method they can is reasonable and fair, they maintain.

The American press, in its coverage, was unable to refer to the cause of the tragedy of the Achille Lauro. But the Italian report pointed again and again to the cause of the tragedy, namely, the homelessness of the Palestinians, as the cause of terrorism inflicted on the Italian boat.

*   *   *

In America, "Jewish-Zionist-Israeli" activities are on a larger scale, more dramatic and are offered with "proper" presentation to the news media. Therefore, news concerning Israel, Zionism and Jews at large receives greater coverage and is considered more "newsworthy."

But beyond this understandable ground for the greater presentation of Israeli and Jewish news, there is the "favorable" presentation and "distortion." There are hundreds of "talk shows" on American radio and television stations. There are tens upon tens of Zionist and pro-Israeli hosts on these talk shows. Many of these hosts choose mainly pro-Israeli guests and present pro-Israeli positions. There are hardly any Arab and Muslim talk show hosts to sympathize with

14

the other viewpoints and present a balanced position on the issues of the Middle East.

The author recalls that some 25 years ago, when on an exceptional occasion a talk show host would invite him to appear on the program because he (the author) had, literally, imposed himself on the station and the media as a newsworthy spokesman, he would be confronted invariably by four or five Zionist pro-Israelis and one or two Israelis. Even as of mid-1986, he was invited to appear on a television program in New York City and was surrounded by Zionist guests. To his left was a prominent Zionist radio personality and to his right was another Zionist claiming to be an "expert on the Middle East." There was a woman guest who was also pro-Israel. And the host of the show was, you guessed it, a strong, pro-Israel Zionist!

The American people, in the main, receive a one-sided presentation and interpretation of Mideast news and events, including the issue of terrorism. The press is, as a rule, pro-Israel, pro-colonialism and racism, and pro-*status quo*, generally opposed to change. This one-sided presentation denies the American people the opportunity to examine other people's interpretations of terrorism and what makes a person a terrorist.

Briefly, Americans are opposed to terrorism without knowing what it is or what causes it, as they know very little about the world and what makes international politics. When USS Stark was hit in May 1987 in the Persian Gulf and scores of American sailors were killed, the majority of Americans did not know where the Gulf was!

* * *

As explained, it is no surprise that the American people at large have very little understanding of the world community. But what is surprising is the fact that the American government misunderstands so much.

When the United States attacked Libya, there was a simplistic belief in the White House that the attack might encourage the military dissidents in Libya to engage in a *coup* against Qaddafi and overthrow the man. Failing to understand the simple human reaction that when there is a foreign attack, people would rally around their beleaguered leader, the White House expressed several times the hope that Qaddafi might have been killed by internal opposing factions.

Later, the White House claimed that Qaddafi's powers had been clipped by the Revolutionary Command Council. This, of course, was wishful thinking, or was it disinformation? The White House also has another simplistic notion that if Qaddafi disappears, terrorism will come to an end. But if this Qaddafi is killed, there will be another Qaddafi and a third Qaddafi and a tenth Qaddafi. As long as the cause that creates "terrorism" exists in the Middle East, "Qaddafis" will appear again and again.

Another misconception was based on the assumption that Qaddafi was the orchestra leader of world terrorism. He would tell the terrorist organizations of the world to stop and they would. Or ask them to engage in acts of terrorism and they would start. The misconception in Washington that the elimination of Qaddafi would eliminate the cause of violence, was as shallow as the general thinking of uninformed people everywhere.

Political decisions made by Americans affect the lives and destinies of other nations. Yet those nations have no way to affect the American decision-making process even if those decisions are to the detriment of the people in the countries abroad!

The late Robert Kennedy, of course, did not hate the Arabs and, possibly, he did not love the Jews. But in the 1967–68 elections, he was willing to offer 50 phantom jets to Israel in order to win some 50,000 Jewish votes. Those phantom jets, given to Israel, would someday kill Arabs, as they indeed did many a time, later.

Robert Kennedy, of course, was not interested in killing Arabs. But his action in the course of the elections resulted in the death of thousands of Arabs. Indeed, Robert Kennedy can be considered as the man responsible for the arms race in the Middle East. The Israeli occupation of Sinai, annexation of the Golan Heights and war in Lebanon might be traced to Bobby Kennedy's desire to become the President of the United States.

On June 5, 1968, Sirhan Bishara Sirhan committed a terrible crime by shooting the presidential candidate, Robert F. Kennedy. Was Sirhan able to appeal to Kennedy in any way whatever so that politician Kennedy would not push for giving phantom jets to Israel? In Sirhan's own words, if he had wanted "to lick Kennedy's boots, pleading with him not to send the phantom jets to Israel, Kennedy would not have even stopped to have his boots licked" by Sirhan.

Sirhan, of course, committed an act of terrorism. But Robert Kennedy's pushing for arms to Israel has led to hundreds of acts committed by Israeli terrorists, resulting in the death of tens of thou-

16

sands of Palestinians, Syrians, Lebanese and other Arabs. Kennedy was responsible for acts of war terrorism and other horrors in the Middle East.

Sirhan, of course, could have appealed to the American people to pressure Kennedy not to send arms to Israel. But in the absence of the capability to affect American public opinion peacefully to prevent Kennedy from supporting Israel, an act of terrorism was committed by Sirhan in reaction to Kennedy's promotion of war in the Middle East. This, of course, does not justify Sirhan's terrible act. It is, rather, an explanation of why such horrible acts take place. If we understand the cause of terrorism, we may be able to prevent future horrors.!

Because America is the most powerful country in the world, Americans feel that they are also the wisest and most knowledgeable. But power does not necessarily mean wisdom and, while the U.S. has the strongest air force, Mr. Reagan is not the personification of wisdom in the world. Most assuredly, he is not the policeman of the world and he cannot eliminate terrorism by police actions taken unilaterally or even in concert with European powers.

* * *

The foreign policy of the United States is based on two simplistic assumptions: the "Shah" syndrome and the syndrome of militarism.

The "Shah" syndrome. As Americans love to be loved, they try to depend on the "good boys" of the world, those who say they are "pro-Americas," as explained earlier. These "good boys" include Trojillo, Batista, Somoza, Marcos, Duvalier, the Shah of Iran, Sadat of Egypt and others. In the past the list included Chaing Kai Chek, Sygman Rhee of South Korea, Diem of South Vietnam, Franco of Spain, Salazar of Portugal and other anti-communist dictators and tyrants.

Take the case of the Shah of Iran. America supported Mohammed Reza Pahlevi and alienated the people of Iran. Naturally, governments must deal with governments and cannot deal with "people." But, while the U.S. should not have direct dealings with the people of Iran and other countries, it should not support tyrannical rulers of such lands against the people of those lands.

In the case of Sadat of Egypt, Americans were all excited that the Egyptian leader was willing to sell what he did not own, the rights of the people of Palestine, exactly like the man who sold the Brooklyn

17

Bridge! He was praised in the American press and became a star of American television. If he had run for the presidency of the United States, he would have had greater support than any American politician, including Jimmy Carter.

It didn't bother the American people or their government that Sadat was a tyrant who had imprisoned a large segment of Egyptian intellectuals, college professors, journalists and writers. However, Americans were shocked when Sadat was shot. Whether Sadat was "assassinated" or "executed" was a question that the Americans never bothered to examine. In the Arab world, the death of Sadat did not bring too many tears to the eyes of the people, even though the Americans were more mournful and tearful on that occasion. So who was wrong—the Arab peoples' attitude toward Sadat or the attitude of the Americans from a distance, without a knowledge of what Sadat had done and how he had kept himself in power?

Imagine, if you can, the American President flying to Tokyo after Pearl Harbor in the interest of peace with the Japanese aggressors. In the process, and in the interest of peace, he offers Canada as a payment to the Japanese so that peace will be established in the Pacific. All this flight to Tokyo and the giving of Canada to the Japanese "in the interest of peace" takes place without the knowledge of the U.S. Senate or the American people or authorization of the people of Canada. Imagine, if you can, what the attitude of the people in North America would be toward such an American President who is seeking peace with the Japanese.

This was exactly what Sadat did, flying to Jerusalem without any authority from the people of Palestine or the Arabs or even the Egyptian people. There, he offered Palestine to become a legitimate Jewish state and recognized the occupation of that land by the Jews of Europe, America and elsewhere. Of course, this was in the interest of peace, similar to the American President flying to Tokyo in the interest of peace! No wonder the Arab people resented Sadat and resented the American support of Sadat.

The military syndrome is also linked to the Shah syndrome. America's obsession with militarism, military aid and military solutions to political and economic problems was clear at Camp David. As a result of Camp David, the United States gave Israel $3 billion and $2 billion was offered to Egypt. When the $2 billion is divided by 40 million Egyptians, every Egyptian receives $200. And when the $3 billion is divided by 3 million Israelis, every Israeli receives $1,000.

The $2 billion to Egypt included $1.8 billion military aid and only $200 million economic aid. And when that $200 million economic aid is divided by the 40 million Egyptians, every poor Egyptian receives $5.00 for his economic well-being. To Israel, the U.S. gave $3 billion, of which $2.2 billion was in military aid to keep the Jewish state stronger than all the Arabs. It included $800 million in economic aid. When this $800 million is divided by the 3 million Israelis, every Israeli receives $270, in contrast to the $5 received by every Egyptian.

No wonder the people of Egypt and the Arab world were not unhappy when Sadat disappeared from the scene. And no wonder the Arabs' animosity toward America increased, despite the $5 billion lost to America; it brought no peace to the Middle East.

Indeed, as a result of the Camp David accord, which strengthened Israeli military power and made the United States directly involved in the military aspects of the Mideast problem, the Israelis annexed the Golan Heights of Syria, paving the road for the Greater Israel and greater wars. On June 6, 1982, Israel attacked Lebanon, rampaging that poor land and creating more hatred toward America. The shattered families and destroyed refugee camps became the breeding ground for individuals who lost their mothers, children, sisters, fathers. These were killed or maimed by American bombs, napalms and American cluster bombs. They became nihilists who considered life meaningless and, therefore, were ready to consider all Americans responsible for their tragedy and legitimate targets to be attacked anywhere.

It is there, in those refugee camps, that the root of recent Palestinian "terrorism" should be found.

Chapter II

Terrorism and War

It has been stated that what is considered as "terrorism" by one party may be considered as an act of "patriotism" by another. But we should go beyond this. "Terrorism is an act of war" and "war is an act of terrorism." Terrorism is the instrument of war carried out by the weak; whereas the strong will use war, which of course, is an act of terrorism.

Both "terrorism" and "war" use force and violence in order to impose the will of the employer of that force on the other party. The object of the violence is human beings and property. Violence is usually employed in a sudden way, the element of surprise being an important device to subjugate the will of the other party. The American planes which attacked Tripoli and Benghazi did their violent action at 2:00 A.M. when people were asleep and not expecting bombs to be dropped on them.

The "terrorists" kill five, ten or 20 persons. But those who engage in acts of "war-terrorism" kill hundreds or thousands and destroy property worth millions of dollars. The horrors of war-terrorism are more damaging and more evil than the horrors of simple terrorism. Yet in terms of "civilized" behavior, we have been conditioned to denounce "terrorism" and give war a place of honor! Of course, both terrorism and war have their own rules. Both are against the killing of children and the weak, even though in reality both war and terrorism have children and the weak as their victims.

In the Palestinian terrorist attack on the Rome airport, there was one 11 year-old American girl killed. This was well publicized in the American press. But during the Israeli attack on Lebanon in June 1982, ʔ   ̔ 1 year-old Palestinian and Lebanese girls were killed and burnt ʋ   ̔th by the American airplanes, tanks, bombs and napalm which were given to and used by the Israelis. The deaths of those 285 11 year-old girls was at least as much of a horror as the death of the one 11 year-old American girl. Yet the American press made no mention of the Palestinian and Lebanese 11 year-old girls. And so "terrorism" depends, to a great extent, on the publicity given to the horrible act. If the acts of war are equally publicized as brutal, evil and bloody examples of murder, then people will consider war an even greater horror than simple acts of terrorism.

On the other hand, if sufficient analysis is made as to the reasons terrorists commit terrorism, then the people will somehow understand the cause and motivation of the terrorists. And, therefore, their acts will be found less irrational, even though equally abhorrent. As the result, efforts might be directed to eliminate the cause.

People consider war less abhorrent due to the whole process of rationalization and justification of why a nation is engaged in war. Hence, war becomes somehow more acceptable. Those who commit "terrorism" have not attempted to explain their cause in order to gain "acceptability," as those who engage in war-terrorism have.

Terrorists are not born; circumstances create terrorists. So what are the causes and circumstances that have created terrorists and what are the goals of the terrorists? These questions must be thoroughly examined and studied if the purpose is to eliminate terrorism. Regretfully, within the American scene today hardly any attention is given to the "cause" of terrorism and efforts are invariable directed at simply condemning terrorism. Indeed, on the radio and television talk shows, the hosts invariably shut up the guests who might try to discuss the cause.

Condemning terrorism is so simple and so useless! As James Reston observed many years ago, it is easy to condemn evil, but it is far more important to examine the cause of the evil act. Later we shall discuss at some length the causes of Arab terrorism as the case study, with references to other "terrorist" acts carried out by other groups.

Without discovering the cause of terrorism and eliminating the cause, there is no possibility that terrorism will be eliminated. Nevertheless, there are two broad schools of thought on how to react toward terrorism even before getting to its root cause.

The practice in America on the domestic level provides us with one "model." Whenever there are terrorists who are holding hostages in a bank or a house or a school, the first thing that police do is to establish lines of communication. They will provide the terrorists and the hostage holders with telephone lines, and in New York and elsewhere a "hostage-negotiating team" has been set, ready for such crises.

The teams have developed special techniques and finesse in discussing and communicating with the hostage holders. The police teams try to learn the gripes of the kidnapper and the cause of his frustration and how and to what extent those demands can be met. Such negotiations go on for a day or two or as long as possible so that, ultimately, the hostages, as well as the hostage holders, are released safely.

This technique has been very successful almost everywhere throughout the United States. Of course, there are exceptions, but the exceptions are there to prove the rule, namely, the shortest and most peaceful road to salvaging such a crisis situation is through communication and negotiation.

This method of negotiation was even carried out on the international scene by the Carter Administration. President Carter, despite all difficulties, pressures and humiliations, was able to stand up and negotiate for 444 long days to get the American hostages in the U.S. Embassy safely out of Teheran. The pressures on Carter to use force were unlimited and, even though he was tempted once to do so, he recognized the futility of that method and resorted once more to the peaceful device of negotiation.

In the election contest with Ronald Reagan, a super-patriot who was willing to endanger the lives of the American hostages in order to save face for America, Carter resisted the pressures and, indeed, possibly jeopardized his own second term presidency. His commitment to the saving of the lives of the hostages was stronger than his commitment to saving face and his own political career.

Was that a sign of weakness on the part of Carter and American willpower? Or was it the proof of the real strength of the President and the American society he was leading? History will give the man from Georgia greater credit than his detractors have offered today.

President Reagan represents the opposite philosophy. To him, there is "no negotiation with terrorists." He would rather send the Marines or the sixth Fleet or the Air Force, killing and destroying, than negotiating or recognizing the "terrorists" and their claims and arguments as to their rights. The use of force against the "terrorists" rather than negotiation is the policy of the Reagan Administration.

Of course, there are terrorists and terrorists. President Reagan, who is against terrorism, supports, at least with the $100 million he has requested from Congress, the terrorist "contras" of Nicaragua. He supported Marcos before the people of the Philippines overthrew him, as he supported Duvalier of Haiti before his overthrow by the people. In mid-1987, the greatest act of terrorism is carried out everyday in South Africa, where tens upon tens of people are being killed by the white, racist regime. Despite minor disagreements with President Botha, Reagan is supportive of his regime.

But Reagan has his opposition to Muammar Qaddafi of Libya and occasionally he talks tough against the President of Syria and Khomeini of Iran as sponsors of terrorism. However, in reality, it is possible that Syria, Iran, North Korea and Russia support "terrorism" more than Libya. Indeed, President Reagan's support of the "contras" promotes "terrorism" more than all others.

There are at least 125 "terrorist" organizations in the world. It should be noted that members of these organizations describe themselves as "freedom fighters" or "liberation movements." Each organization has its own agenda and is independent of the others. Occasionally they work with each other. But sometimes they even work against each other. Some of them might get funding and training in Libya; others receive their support from other sources. But they all act independently, accordingly to their own different plans, goals and agendas.

There are "terrorist" organizations of the right (white, racist groups in southern states and in Idaho, for example.) And there are "terrorist" organizations of the left. There are individual "terrorists" (freelance terrorists) and "terrorists" who are engaged on the basis of contracts.

Some "terrorist" organizations have ideological backgrounds on the basis of which they proceed with their acts of terrorism until their goals have been achieved (such as the Mau Mau in Kenya or the Jewish terrorists in Palestine).

In recent years, these "terrorist" organizations have included the Irish Republican Army, Baader-Meinhof, Red Brigade, Palestine Liberation Organization (with its many factions), African National Congress (and the People's Congress), the Red Army, etc. Qaddafi is not the general director of all these groups, but the White House does not understand this simple fact.

The U.S. attack on Qaddafi was conceived by these organizations as an attack on them all. It brought them together and strengthened their resolve to carry out their plans and goals. Qaddafi might provide some aid to the African National Congress and to the P.L.O. However, he cannot order these organizations to deviate from their own goals, the liberation of their lands.

The problem is in the perception of terrorism. Reagan believes that he is the man in charge of the "good" deeds in the world as against the evil-doers of the world. And so his acts are wholesome, even if they lead to the death and destruction of hundreds and thousands, whereas the reaction of other people to America and America's "allies" represents evil and terrorism.

Mr. Reagan considers Muammar Qaddafi of Libya as the chief promoter of terrorism in the world. He has directed his words of condemnation, as well as his military might, against Libya and the Libyan leader.

Mr. Reagan considers Libya to be an "extraordinary" threat to the national security of the United States. Either Reagan is exaggerating out of proportion and presenting an unreasonable argument to the American people concerning Qaddafi's threat, or the United States is, indeed, that weak and that incompetent so that Libya, with its 2.5 million population, can pose as an extraordinary threat to America.

If the President's Executive Order against travel to Libya is based on such an unreasonable assumption, it would have to be rendered by the Supreme Court as unconstitutional. On the assumption that the Executive Order was an unconstitutional abridgment of the right to travel and freedom of speech guaranteed by the First Amendment, the author left for Libya in January 1986 in defiance of that Order and to reaffirm the right of the citizen to travel and to freedom of speech. In Libya he met with Muammar Qaddafi, the chief promoter of world terrorism, according to Mr. Reagan.

So who is this Muammar Qaddafi?

Qaddafi is not as great as his supporters believe nor as bad as President Reagan and the American press paint. He is an Arab intellectual of a sort who has written a booklet presenting a few thoughts concerning the world community. His ideas are a mixture of Islamic teachings, a bit of socialism, anarchism and western democracy.

As an intellectual, he is not on the level of a David Hume or Alexander Hamilton. But in his emotional hopes for the future and his passionate opposition to every form of foreign tyrannical rule, he is not too dissimilar from a young, emotional Virginian.

That Virginian declared in the House of Burgesses in Williamsburg during the colonial period that he was so opposed to the British rule that he would put the British Isles on a boat, take it to the middle of the Atlantic Ocean and sink them. It was the more seasoned and mature George Washington who rebuked the young man, "Mr. Jefferson, there is one problem. You do not have large enough boats on which to put the British islands to bring them to the middle of the ocean."

Differently stated, the emotional Qaddafi has a long road in the process of growing up before he reaches a more seasoned position and views the world community with a more balanced attitude, as did Jefferson.

At any rate, Qaddafi's pamphlet, "The Green Book," contains some interesting thoughts, such as *albaito le sakeneh* ("the house belongs to its dweller.") And there are many simplistic thoughts, such as *man tahazzaba khan* ("participation in political parties is equivalent to treason"). Accordingly, there is only one political party in the whole of Libya. It is the People's Congress and there is no "government" in "al-Jamahiryyah" ("the country of the masses") on the simple theory that the people rule themselves and, hence, there is no need or place for government.

Qaddafi thinks that these ideas are the ultimate contribution to reflective thinking and the creation of the "Just Society." Recognizing that Qaddafi's and his people's belief that "The Green Book" is the best book is unreasonable, still it does not make the Libyan leader the world's chief terrorist.

Qaddafi observed many years ago, "The people who do not produce sufficient foodstuff for themselves are not a free people." To this effect, he has been trying to improve the economic life of the people of Libya, to make them self-sufficient.

He has engaged in a vast irrigation plan, "The Great Man-Made River Project," in which some $3.5 billion was invested by the people to bring water from about 500 miles away in the desert to the population centers along the coast in Benghazi and Tripoli. Economic progress and land reform are taking place in Libya. Upon Libyan independence in 1951, there was only one Libyan college graduate. By now there are seven universities in Libya, increasing in number and expanding in student population.

Having been under the terrible colonial rule of fascist Italy, the Libyans, including Qaddafi, are extremely bitter and hostile to colonialism. During the effort to attain their freedom, the Libyans lost about one million human beings out of a population of two million. This explains Libyan support for freedom in South Africa, for the liberation of the people of the Philippine Islands from the corrupt rule of Marcos or the Haitians from Duvalier or the Palestinians from Zionist occupation. This anti-colonialism is a very strong and powerful feeling in Libya, just as it is in the rest of the Arab and Third World countries. But Libyan experience under fascist rule gives Libyans possibly a more distinguished position in opposition to colonialism than most other peoples in the Third World.

Qaddafi is not John Stewart Mill nor Roger Baldwin, in any sense of the word. He is, like most leaders in the Third World, an autocratic ruler who believes in a one-party system. Within the party, there is all the freedom of assembly and freedom of speech. The direction of the meetings and the nature of the issues to be debated are suggested by the leader himself. The Libyan experiment is not similar to American democracy, but then the Third World, as a whole, is in the process of democratization, which may take 100 more years, just as the process has taken the West some 400 or 500 years.

Libya and the Arab and Third Worlds are, in an historic perspective, in the revolutionary stage of the American and Western experiment. And, thus, Libya supports the liberation movements against colonial rules in Palestine and South Africa and earlier in Rhodesia (Zimbabwe) and other African colonial territories. It also has supported revolutionary movements in many other parts of the world. These "revolutionary movements" or "freedom fighters," in the vocabulary of the Libyans, Arabs and Third World people, are decried in western vocabulary as "terrorists."

President Reagan has described Muammar Qaddafi as the "mad dog of the East." If Qaddafi's efforts to make his country self-sufficient, to produce foodstuff and not have to depend on the import of wheat from abroad, and if his support of national liberation movements makes him a "mad dog," then it will be in order to examine the validity of Mr. Reagan's remark.

In the first place, it is "unpresidential" for the head of a civilized superpower to use those words, describing the head of another state. Those are the words of truck drivers, talking to each other in an angry language, not the president of a great power talking about the head of state of another country.

This type of unbecoming language is a habit with the Reagan Administration. In Tokyo, Secretary of State George Schultz spoke of the 1986 Tokyo Declaration Against Terrorism and addressed himself to Qaddafi, "You've had it, pal!" Again, this is not the language of the Secretary of State of a great power. "You've had it, pal!" is the common spoken language of taxi drivers in New York City. The Reagan Administration briefly, in its obsession with terrorism, has, amongst other things, lowered the standards of the debate in the country. That is not good for the Administration, nor will it adversely affect terrorism in the world.

The President has referred to Qaddafi as "flaky." Indeed, in many parts of the United States, Americans somehow believe that Qaddafi is an unbalanced person because that is what the President said and that is what the news media has circulated. However, where the other 85 percent of the world population lives, in New Delhi, Nairobi, Jakarta or Accra, if one asks who is "flaky"—Qaddafi or Reagan—it must be reported with regret that Mr. Reagan will win by a landslide. Also, if the people in the countries comprising that seven-eighths of the human race are asked who is supporting terrorism and promoting terrorism and who is the chief terrorist in the world, the answer will be Reagan of the United States much more frequently than Qaddafi of Libya.

The American people will be astonished to hear of these reactions among 85 percent of the human race. They have been telling each other they're good, the others are evil. American reporters and commentators on radio and television have been reaffirming, in the main, the conviction that the Americans are right, the rest of the people of the world are wrong. However, it is in order for Americans, who claim they are the leaders of the world, to really become acquainted with the feelings of the majority of the people of the world to be good leaders!

During his meeting with Qaddafi in Tripoli, the author asked the Libyan leader about his support of the revolutionary movements. Qaddafi's answer was a definite "Yes, support for revolutions for freedom always and everywhere!" Would he have supported the American Revolution? "Of course," Qaddafi replied and then, with a wink, he said, "Listen, doktor, I doubt that your American President of today would have supported the American Revolution of 1776."

What America today considers terrorism is considered by the majority of the people of the world as acts of freedom fighters. In his day, King George III viewed the American War of Independence as acts of violence carried out by American rebels and terrorists.

Moorhead Kennedy, one of the former hostages at the American Embassy in Teheran, summarizes the problem of terrorism in these words: "To understand terrorism, look at the American role abroad."

Today (1987) the government of the United States supports, by and large, the government of Botha in South Africa. In a few years, the white, racist regime in that land will disappear and the majority will form the government in the spirit of democracy. "Azania" will replace "South Africa," just as Zimbabwe replaced Rhodesia. At present, however, the government of Botha receives its inspiration from the United States and Israel. When Botha attacked three frontline African countries in hot pursuit to fight "terrorism," he invoked the American and Israeli examples. The attacks by Israel on Tunis (some 1,500 miles away), and by the United States on Tripoli and Benghazi (some 5,000 miles away from American shores) were invoked as precedents for his aggression against the three neighboring states.

Was Botha engaged in "terrorism" or "war" and was the United States engaged in "war" or "terrorism" when it attacked Libya? And when Israel attacked Lebanon, was it engaged in "terrorism" or "war"?

War is terrorism and terrorism is war.

Chapter III

Terrorism: Who Pays?

We should, of course, condemn simple terrorism no less than condemning war-terrorism. But, as stated earlier, to condemn evil is so easy and so useless! We must stop war and stop terrorism. Indeed we must stop wars in order to stop terrorism.

To prevent wars, universal and total disarmament should be the goal of every civilized person. Presently, the United States spends some $400 billion for arms every year and the Soviets do a similar evil thing, too. The two superpowers can destroy the world several times over and yet no serious effort has been made to rescue the human race from these powers. Indeed, the protection of the "underdeveloped" Third World people from the horrors of the technologically "overdeveloped" superpowers is the prime goal of the Third World intelligensia and should be the goal of the Western intellectuals.

When wars, proxy wars, and acts of oppression come to an end, terrorism will die automatically, no doubt.

However, until that happy day when there will be war no more, there will be many cases of "terrorism." What to do, then, about terrorism in the meantime?

It was mentioned in the previous chapter that there are two broad methods of dealing with terrorism: the school that advocates "negotiation" and those who believe in "the use of force." Israel is the arch-prototype of the second school. Indeed, the permanent Israeli representative to the United Nations, Benjamin Netanyaho, has written a book entitled *Terrorism: How the West Can Win.*

Mr. Netanyaho appears on American radio and television stations whenever there is something related to Israel, Zionism or Jews. And, of course, almost everything is related to the "Jewish question."

He speaks English with an impeccable American pronunciation because the "Israeli" Ambassador is an American from Shaker Heights, Ohio. He went to Israel, renounced his American citizenship and became an instant Israeli. No wonder he speaks with no foreign accent!

Another personal note about Benjamin Netanyaho. His brother, Jonathan also from Ohio, renounced his U.S. citizenship too, and in

Entebee, Uganda, he killed some 10 to 15 Arabs, Jews and Ugandans before he, too, was shot dead. The American press never refers to the Netanyahos as having been Americans who renounced their U.S. citizenship nor does the press ever mention that Jonathan Netanyaho killed some 10 to 15 person before he was shot to death!

Benjamin Netanyaho maintains that most acts of terrorism are carried out by governments either directly by their agents or through subcontractors. He claims, for example, that Abu Nidal works for the governments of Syria and Libya "on a time-sharing basis." Therefore, attacking such governments is the first priority in the process of stopping terrorism.

The embassies of such governments should be shut down, he states. These embassies are vital for the conduct of the terrorists' war in Europe. Furthermore, these countries should be denied landing rights in European airports and economic sanctions should be imposed upon them. Also, when necessary, military actions should be taken against these governments, Natanyaho maintains.

Israel always responds to terrorism and has made it clear to the governments that are involved in terrorism that there is a price to pay, the Israeli official declares. The response can be a combination of economic pressure, diplomatic pressure and, in some instances, military action.

According to Netanyaho, Israel views the war on terrorism as a "comprehensive, continuous campaign against the source of terror." That does not mean taking action after each incident. But, ultimately, pressure should be brought on those regimes which support terrorism. To do that effectively, the West, which is the target of terrorism, has to do it in concert, he states.

Netanyaho was pleased with Reagan's attack on Libya and his efforts to involve the Western Europeans in developing sanctions against Qaddafi. Informed on the "Larry King Live" television show that some 1.8 million Americans had cancelled or changed their travel plans to Europe for fear of terrorist attacks, the American-born Israeli representative snapped back, "We should not let Qaddafi be our travel agent!" He added, "Terrorism is a phenomenon that tries to evoke one basic feeling—fear."

"But you have to muster the courage of a society. The only antithesis or the only response to terrorism is, in fact, the opposite of fear. And that's courage," he declared.

"In Israel we have adopted a combination of measures which we advocate. That is, a combination of preventive measures to make it hard for the terrorists to strike at us and offensive measures in which we go after the concentrations of terror and we take those kinds of actions that prevent them from attacking us," Netanyaho explained.

"The Soviet Union has been the big brother of terrorism. It's been the behind-the-scene force that encouraged these regimes and these groups; the P.L.O. trained in the Soviet Union, along with terrorists from many other countries, from Latin America, from Africa and elsewhere and Europe. The Soviet Union has found in terrorism the way that the radical Arab states have found in terrorism—a useful and, until recently, a cost-free way of waging political warfare against the west," according to Netanyaho.

Of course, Netanyaho is correct in his observation that the terrorists intend to invoke the feeling of fear. He should know! In Palestine, the chief Jewish terrorist of his day, Menachim Begin, successfully employed terror against the Arabs and invoked fear and panic which led to the Palestinian refugee exodus of 1948.[6]

But the belief of the Israelis in force as the primary device against Palestinian Arab "terrorism" has deeper roots.

The persecuted, paradoxically admires and usually tries to imitate his PROSECUTOR! In his *True Believer*, Eric Hoffer explains this phenomenon at some length. In psychological terms this is called "displacement" or "identification with the aggressor" syndrome. The Jews in Palestine, having been persecuted by the more powerful Fascist and Nazis forces in Europe, recognized the significance of "power" and what it can do. This recognition made the persecuted appreciative of the use of power. Upon attaining a measure of power in Palestine, the Palestinian Jews applied that power effectively and amongst other things evicted the Palestinian Arabs. The persecuted in Europe became the new Prosecutor in Palestine.

Hence Israel's belief in force and the use of force has its roots in the horror and persecution inflicted upon the Jews in Europe and the West. Thus, the Palestinians became the victims of the victims of Western anti-Semitism.

At any rate, the Israeli approach, which is now being followed by the Reagan Administration, i.e., that there shall be no negotiation with terrorists, has brought more death and destruction than the Israelis are willing to admit. From Karyat Shemona to Entebbe to the Munich tragedy to the attack on Lebanon on June 6, 1982, a high

31

price was paid by the Israelis, possibly higher than the price paid by the "terrorists." This the Israelis never admit!

To the hostage-takers, the hostages are their protection and security. The Israelis invariably decide to attack the school, the bus or the airplane in which hostages are held. This will endanger the lives of their own students, passengers and athletes, as it eliminates the protection for the hostage-holders. The kidnappers, having lost their hostages (their security), will have no reason not to use force. The result is a shoot out in which everybody, or almost all persons involved, will be killed by the fire of the rescuer-attackers and the kidnappers.

This was vivid in Munich. The Palestinians invaded the Israeli Village at the 1972 Olympics site and captured some Israeli athletes and held them hostage. Who were these "Israeli" athletes? One of them, David Berger, was from Shaker Heights, Ohio, USA.[7] Another "Israeli" was from Poland. The third "Israeli" was from Hungary. The fifth "Israeli" was from Russia and one was from Rumania.

These "Israelis" from various countries of the world had gone to Palestine and occupied that land, the land of the Palestinian "terrorists." Many a time, the Palestinians had attempted to return to their own villages in Palestine, but the European and American "Israelis" would not permit them to return and would shoot them if they tried. The Palestinian "terrorists," having been denied by the Israeli occupiers the normal, human right to return to their own villages peacefully, had no alternative but to go to the "Israeli" Village in the Munich Olympics forcefully.

And what was the purpose of the Palestinians? Their purpose was to dramatize their cause and gain certain concessions that they would eventually be able to return to their land. The Israeli Government would not permit such a thing, with its theory of not giving in to terrorism. It was under the order of the Israeli Government of Golda Meir and Moshe Dayan that the Israeli and Western German sharpshooters attacked the helicopter which was about to carry the Israeli hostages and their Palestinian kidnappers at the Munich airport. That shooting led finally to the death of all the athletes and all the Palestinians.

In a court of law, the Palestinians might be charged with kidnapping, but Golda Meir would be charged with ordering to kill and murder. At any rate, the Israelis did not negotiate and used force. If the Palestinians had succeeded and flown out of Munich with their hostages, they might have won some political concessions, but the athletes would have been alive. But Israel did not negotiate and paid a high price.

Israel's spectacular success at Entebbe had its victims, of course. However, the "success" was possible primarily because of the clumsy training of the Ugandan army. If the Ugandans were properly trained, they would have not permitted a single Israeli to land, much less let them leave the Ugandan airport alive. Again, the use of force, even if successful, is a losing proposition. There were several Jews, Arabs and many Ugandans killed for no good reason. The hostages could have been freed with patience and through negotiation.

In the case of Lebanon, Israel attacked that poor, unhappy country in June 1982 in order to "eliminate terrorism." The Israelis used 1,000 American tanks, several hundred American airplanes and thousands of tons of American bombs. They killed some 20,000 to 30,000 Palestinians, Lebanese and other Arabs, and wounded some 20,000 to 30,000 people, rendering one half of Lebanon destroyed. The Israeli casualties included some 2,000 killed and several thousand wounded. This high price in Arab and Jewish lives was in fulfillment of the theory of "force, not negotiation" with the terrorists.

The so-called Palestinian terrorists, for one year prior to June 6, 1982, had sent their rockets across the Lebanese border to Israel and during the whole period had killed only one individual Israeli, according to David Shipler of *The New York Times*. Shipler also reported that the Palestinian rockets thrown to Israel were in retaliation for Israeli bombings of Palestinian camps in Lebanon.

The death and injury to some 2,000 to 3,000 Israelis and some 20,000 to 40,000 Arabs was much too high a price to pay in pursuit of the theory of "no negotiation." The theory is based on emotional nationalism rather than objective evaluation.

On the basis of one Israeli killed by Palestinian "terrorists" per year, it would take 2,000 to 3,000 years to kill the same number as were killed in Lebanon from June to September 1982. If 10 Israelis were killed by Palestinian rockets per year, it would take 200 to 300 years!

The "no negotiation" theory reflects the behavior of the neurotic and deranged, who apply irrational emotion at the expense of rational thinking and analysis. Reagan's America is exhibiting those symptoms.

The United States is following the Israeli philosophy and uses force rather than negotiation to eliminate terrorism. This is a double-edged sword. It may give some vent to the American national desire for revenge, but it also invites greater acts of violence and damage to the reputation of the United States as a country with the official policy of committing terrorism. Henry Kissinger was responsible for much of this policy.

When America engaged in air piracy and forced a civilian Egyptian plane to change its course and land in Sicily on the assumption that there were "terrorists" on board, America became a skyjacker no better than those who had seajacked the Italian boat, Achille Lauro. America had taken the law into its own hands and, thereby, established a dangerous precedent, enabling any country in the future to divert any civilian airplane on the assumption that there are terrorists on that airplane. Israel has engaged several times in such skyjackings.

And when the United States attacked Tripoli and Benghazi in April 1986 in retaliation for what President Reagan claimed was Libyan involvement in a terrorist act on a disco in West Berlin, America was committing a terrorist act worse than the attack on the disco.

To claim that the American action was against terrorism and, therefore, it was a civilized act of warfare, while what might have been done in Athens, Rome, Vienna and the West Berlin disco were acts of terrorism, is an abuse of the language and a device of self-deception.

The American attack did not eliminate terrorism nor even reduce it. However, the cost to America was at least two pilots and more than $250 million, in addition to worldwide condemnation by the people of Europe, Asia, Africa and Latin America.

Was the use of force worth it? What else could America have done? The United States could have gone to the International Court of Justice, to the Security Council of the United Nations, or could have called a conference of Mediterranean powers. It could have negotiated.

Terrorists take the law into their own hands and consider themselves above the law. The United States has been behaving the same way. Reagan has hijacked an Egyptian civilian airplane, attacked the Gulf of Sidra and the cities of Tripoli and Benghazi, and has refused to accept the rule of law and the decisions of the International Court of Justice. Is the United States a terrorist state?

Chapter IV

Palestine is the Issue!

It is not intended here to discuss the complex problem of Palestine and its very many aspects. That would require several volumes. The intention here is to discuss the nature of the crisis, the American role and the relation of the Palestinian tragedy to terrorism.

The question of Palestine refers to the immigration of Jews, Europeans, Americans and others in this century, to Palestine—which had been inhabited by the Palestinians from time immemorial—against the will of the Arab people, but with British and later American and Western support. The conflict in Palestine is not between Arabs and Jews, as commonly considered. It is a conflict between the Arabs and other non-Zionists on the one hand and the Zionist Jews and their supporters on the other.

By the First World War, Palestine along with the rest of the Arab lands was under the rule of the Ottoman Turks. In 1916 the Arabs revolted against the Ottoman Empire in cooperation with the British and the Allied powers. It was the aim of the Arabs to achieve their political freedom and unity after the war. Britain had promised to support this Arab goal. But while on the one hand Britain promised the Arabs through the famous Hussein-MacMahon correspondence to support Arab independence, it entered into the Sykes-Picot accord with France to divide the Arab land. This accord was one of the secret agreements condemned by President Wilson in his Fourteen Points.

Further, Britain in 1917 promised, in the words of the Balfour Declaration, "the establishment in Palestine of a national home" for the Jews. Of course, the Declaration, being a unilateral promise by Britain to the Jews without Palestinian consent, was not binding upon the Palestinians. Britain was nevertheless cognizant of Arab rights and hence the Balfour Declaration contained a most important qualifying clause which, in a sense, rendered the promise null and void.

After viewing with favor the establishment of a Jewish national home in Palestine, the Declaration goes on with the *proviso* " . . . it being clearly understood that nothing shall be done which may prejudice the civil and religious rights" of the Arabs of Palestine or "the rights and political status" of the Jews in other countries. As a matter of fact, the rights of the Palestinians were prejudiced and hence, even the unilateral promise was rendered null and not binding!

At the time of this Declaration, the population of Palestine was 93 percent Moslem and Christian and 7 percent Jewish. In 1922, the total population of Palestine was 752,048: the Jews numbered 83,790, the Christians and Moslems 660,641, with 7,617 others.[8]

In 1919, the General Syrian Congress meeting in Damascus adopted several resolutions, one of which is of particular interest here insofar as it reflects the Arab attitude towards America. After expressing their desire for full and absolute political independence for a united Syria under a constitutional monarch based on democratic principles, the Congress declared:

> We reject the idea of a Mandate as we believe that the Arab inhabitants of Syria are not less fitted or gifted to govern themselves than certain other nations (Bulgarians, Serbs, Rumanians) when granted independence. If, however, the Paris peace conference should insist on establishing a Mandate, we ask the United States of America to be the mandatory power, for a period not exceeding 20 years, and if the U.S.A. should find herself unable to accede to our request for assistance, then Great Britain should be given the Mandate.

When a people as intensely nationalistic and proud as the Arabs express their willingness to place their future in the hands of America, that is a great tribute to America and its people.

The General Syrian Congress also expressed its attitude toward Zionism and the Jewish "national home":

> We reject the claims of the Zionists for the establishment of a Jewish Commonwealth in that part of Southern Syria which is known as Palestine, and we are opposed to Jewish immigration into any part of the country. We do not acknowledge that they have a title, and we regard their claims as a grave menace to our national, political and economic life. Our Jewish fellow-citizens shall continue to enjoy the rights and to bear the responsibilities which are ours in common.

In accordance with the principle of self-determination which President Wilson had enunciated, he sent a commission to the Middle

East to ascertain the views of the people of the area regarding their future. This was the famous King-Crane Commission, which submitted its report and recommendations in 1919. The Commission recommended in favor of the independence and unity of Syria. On the question of Zionism, the Commission declared:

We recommend serious modification of the extreme Zionist Program for Palestine of unlimited immigration of Jews, looking finally to making Palestine distinctly a Jewish State.

The Commissioners began their study of Zionism with minds predisposed in its favor, but the actual facts in Palestine, coupled with the force of the general principles proclaimed by the Allies and accepted by the Syrians have driven them to the recommendation here made.

A national home for the Jewish people is not equivalent to making Palestine into a Jewish State; nor can the erection of such a Jewish State be accomplished without the gravest trespass upon the civil and religious rights of existing non-Jewish communities in Palestine.

The Commission found that the Zionist program was incompatible with the principle of self-determination and Arab rights:

If the principal of self-determination is to rule and the wishes of Palestine's population are to be decisive as to what is to be done with Palestine, then it is to be remembered that the non-Jewish population of Palestine—nearly nine-tenths of the whole—are emphatically against the entire Zionist program. . .

The Peace Conference should not shut its eyes to the fact that the anti-Zionist feeling in Palestine and Syria is intense and not lightly to be flouted. . .Decisions requiring armies to carry out are sometimes necessary, but they are surely not gratuitously to be taken in the interests of serious injustice. For the initial claim, often submitted by Zionist representatives, that they have a 'right' to Palestine, based on an occupation of 2,000 years ago, can hardly be seriously considered.[9]

Thus as early as 1919 the nature of Zionism, Arab rights and the moral issue involved if Zionist claims were to be materialized were all brought to the attention of the American officials. But if the report did not affect American policy in the Middle East, it is in part at least due to the fact that the report was kept secret until 1922. This was probably due to the disapproval of its contents by Louis Brandeis and Felix Frankfurter and other leading and influential Zionists.

Zionism is a political movement which claims that Palestine belongs to the Jews. The Zionist movement has based its claim on "historical" ground, and appealed to religious and humanitarian sentiments, and applied its political and economic pressure to achieve its aim. The Zionist arguments have been circulated in America so much that almost every American has become familiar with the Zionist position, and due to constant repetition, many have come to accept their validity. But there is another side to the Zionist claims.

The Zionist arguments can be summarized as follows: advancing a special theory of historical "rights", the Zionists' major premise is that Palestine belongs to the Jews because some 3,000 years ago Hebrew tribes from Egypt had conquered that land and established there a state. And as the Jews, according to the Zionists, have been living in exile during the last 2,000 years, they are entitled as a matter of historical "right" to go "back home."

A second supporting argument is offered in the name of the Bible to the effect that God had promised Palestine to the Jews and the Jewish return to Palestine is in fulfillment of Biblical prophecies.

A third supporting argument advanced by the Zionists is that the Jews were persecuted and mistreated in Europe and were in a desperate need for a place of their own. Palestine was such a place.

A fourth argument advanced is that the Jews have improved the land in Palestine better than the Arabs, with the implication that because of this "know-how", the Jews are entitled to the land. In order to give legitimacy to their position, the Zionists refer continuously to the backwardness of the Arabs and the Jewish achievement, that the Jews can teach the Arabs, and can raise the standard of living of the Middle East.

Other arguments by the Zionists with wide circulation in the United States include: (5) that the Jews bought the land in Palestine; and (6) that only Arab feudalists and corrupt government oppose Israel, as progressive Israel poses a threat to Arab feudalism.

The Zionists also argue: (7) that the U.N. created Israel and that the Arabs have opposed the United Nations; (8) that in 1948 the Arabs started the war and attacked Israel; (9) that the Palestinian Arab refugees left Palestine of their own accord or due to instigation by Arab leaders; (10) that the Arab leaders are not resettling the Palestinian refugees in order that they may use them as a political pawn; (11) that Israel is a bastion of democracy and America's "trusted ally;" (12) that the Arabs practice a sort of anti-Semitism by discriminating against American Jews who are forbidden to enter Saudi Arabia.

Then there is (13) the Zionists' "constructive" advice, parroted by the American press: let bygones be bygones—let's forget about the past and go on from here.

And finally there is the argument (14) that "Israel is an accomplished fact. . .it is *there*", an argument which is repeated by American politicians in all their speeches to Zionist groups. The Arabs, accordingly, must recognize Israel as the first step towards peace!

These arguments, perpetuated by the various means of communication, are based either on assumptions unacceptable to the Arabs, (or to the Americans if applied to them) or irrelevant facts and half-truths.

The following brief analysis of these arguments is made not in order to establish the validity of the Arabs' and non-Zionists' position (that will have to be determined by the reader himself), but to point out the fact that there is another side to the story and that the American people as a whole have been denied the opportunity to know of the position of the non-Zionists and their argument against Zionism. Or, more to the point, Americans have been denied the knowledge of the cause of their difficulties in the Arab world and the "why" of terrorism directed at America.

1. *Historical "rights"*—The major Zionist premise is that Palestine belongs to the Jews because Jews used to live in Palestine 2,000 years ago. This is an absurd assumption.

There is no basis in law or logic that would vest any group of people today with rights to other lands on the ground that some people of the claimants' religion or race had conquered that land and occupied it some 3,000 years earlier. To accept the "historical right" theory as the ground for the return of Palestine to the Jews means that similar arguments regarding other people and other lands should be accepted. For example, to accept the Zionist argument that the Jews of today have a right to go to Palestine because it used to belong to some Jews means that we should accept the argument that Alaska belongs to the Russians because it used to belong to them, or that America belongs to the Indians on the ground that it used to belong to the Indians. It is obvious that the acceptance of such arguments would change the whole map of the world. Therefore, we cannot reasonably expect the Palestinian people to accept the Zionist argument that the Jews are going "home" regardless of its romantic appeal to the pro-Zionists.

The Zionist position foments not only Arab resentment, but also the resentment of other peoples. For according to the logic of the "historical rights" of the Zionists, Jews living outside Palestine live in foreign lands and in exile. That is to say, according to Zionism, the Jews in America, England, U.S.S.R., Brazil, India and elsewhere are "Israelis residing in exile." This Zionist position would certainly raise the question of double loyalty of the Zionist Jews. Indeed, the question of double loyalty of the Zionist Jews has been raised by important Zionist leaders. The great Zionist leader and Prime Minister of Israel, Mr. David Ben Gurion, writes in the Israel Government *Yearbook* (1953–54), p. 35:

> When a Jew in America or South Africa speaks of 'our government' to his fellow Jews, he usually means the government of Israel, while the Jewish public in various countries view the Israeli ambassador as their own representative.

This statement either represents the true position and attitude of the Zionist Jews, in which case the charge of double loyalty is a valid statement of fact, or else it does not, and hence it is a wild remark and an attack upon the loyalty of the Jews in America and elsewhere.

It stands to reason that the question of double loyalty advocated by the Zionists jeopardizes the position of the Jews in the Arab lands. If Jews in the Arab countries are "Israelis residing in exile," then certainly they are traitors to the Arabs and at best should be treated as "enemy aliens." Indeed, some of the Jews who had lived in the Arab lands for centuries adhered to the Zionist philosophy and acted as Israelis. This meant that they provided the enemy, from the Arab point of view, with aid and comfort, and as such they could not have been treated by the Arabs except as traitors.

The Arabs had no alternative but to accord these Jewish citizens the status of "enemy aliens" and expel them from the Arab lands. Today the Zionists cry that the Arabs have expelled some of the Jews from the Arab states. But surely the Arabs could not be expected to keep by force a citizen who proclaims his loyalty to the enemy. Indeed, the Arab action was the logical fulfillment of the "historical right" argument and the Zionist premise that the Jews living outside

Palestine are residing in exile. The Zionists could not have it both ways—on the one hand declaring that Jews in the Arab countries and elsewhere were residing in foreign lands which they should abandon and go "home" to Israel, and on the other hand blaming the Arabs for recognizing the logic of the Zionist claim! The Arabs could not be blamed for permitting the "exiles" to depart from the Diaspora and go "home."

Of course not all the Jews believe in the riddle of Zionism. In the United States, the American Jewish Alternatives to Zionism (AJAZ) is dedicated to the proposition that Judaism is a religion of universal values, not a nationality, and that the home of Americans of Jewish faith is America and nowhere else.

2. *Biblical Prophecies*—The Zionists maintain that their historical claim is based on Biblical grounds. Professor Millar Burrows and many other Biblical scholars have pointed out that Genesis XII, 7 "unto thy seed will I give this land," and other Biblical quotations referring to the children of Abraham, include the Arabs, both Moslem and Christian, even perhaps before they include Menachim Begin of Poland or Benjamin Netanyaho of Shaker Heights, Ohio, U.S.A. The fact is that the Arabs, Moslems and Christians are the descendants of the children of Abraham. Accordingly, the Biblical prophecy was fulfilled when Palestine reverted to the "seeds of Abraham" and became an Arab land. With regard to the prophecies concerning the return of the Jews to Palestine, Dr. Alfred Guillaume, Professor of Old Testament Studies at the University of London, writes:

(T)hese prophecies were fulfilled. The Jews did return to Judea, they did rebuild the walls of Jerusalem, and they did rebuild the temple; and after fluctuating fortunes they did secure a brief period of political independence and expansion under the Maccabees. Thus the prophecies of the Return have been fulfilled, and they cannot be fulfilled again. Within the canonical literature of the Old Testament there is no prophecy of a second return after the return from the Babylonian Exile.

Dr. Frank Stagg, Professor of New Testament at the Southern Baptist Theological Seminary in New Orleans, concludes after examining the meaning of "Israel" to the Christian and the allegation that the present day political State of Israel is a step toward the fulfillment of God's work of redemption, that "to identify modern

Israel, the state of the Jewish people, with the 'Israel of God' is to miss the teaching of the New Testament at one of its most vital points."

Refuting the same misconception, the Right Reverend Jonathan G. Sherman, Suffragan Bishop of the Episcopal Diocese of Long Island, writes:

> In the Old Covenant God promised to the children of Israel military victory over their enemies in order that they might enter into the land flowing with milk and honey on the condition of Israel's obedience to his commandments. Israel failed to keep the covenant and so forfeited the promises of God. But God promised a New Covenant, to be written not on tables of stone but in the hearts of his people (Jeramiah 31:31–33; II Corinthians 3:2f). Of this New Covenant Jesus is the mediator (Hebrews 8:6–13; 9:13). In place of victory over human enemies Jesus gives us victory over sin and death (I Corinthians 15:55–57). In place of the land of Canaan he gives us his kingdom (St. Luke 12:32). In place of milk and honey he gives us the fruit of the Spirit—love and joy and peace and forgiveness. Verily, "in him all the promises of God are yes!" (II Corinthians 1:20).

Accordingly, the Bible does not support the Zionist position. Nor do the rules of rational analysis. For it is only reasonable to assume that the Arabs of Palestine are more entitled to their home than Ben Gurion, a Pole, whose ancestors might have been converted to Judaism from amongst some of the Slavic tribes in Eastern Europe several hundred years ago. One wonders whether Palestine is also the home of the ancestors of Elizabeth Taylor and Sammy Davis, Jr., who were recently converted to Judaism!

But even if we assume that Ben Gurion and other Jews were the direct descendants of Abraham, still this does not entitle them to go to the home of the Arab "cousin" without the permission of the "cousin," just as the Americans cannot go to England and Europe on the basis of the historic ties and European ancestry without British and European permission.

Furthermore, the assertion that "the return of the Jews to Palestine is a fulfillment of Biblical prophecy and is based on historical rights" cannot be supported by facts. For the fact is that the Jews have not gone, and are not going, to Palestine unless we consider the 20 percent of world Jewry that lives today in Israel as the majority and the 80 percent of the Jews who have declined the "opportunity" of going to Palestine as an insignificant fraction.

The fact is that the Jews have not gone to Israel and are not going there. There are some 6 million Jews in America and the door is wide open for them to go! Of course the anti-Semites would like very much to ship these American Jews out and send them "home". To be sure such an action will bring the delight and the approval of Israeli leaders, but to say at present that the Jews have gone home or are going home is plainly absurd and without factual foundation.

If Palestine is the home of the Jews, then the American Zionist Jews should certainly go home. That they prefer the status of "exile" reflects upon the peculiarity of Zionism and the absurdity of its arguments.

The absurdity of the Zionist argument becomes completely vivid by further analysis. If the Jews of Shaker Heights have the "right" to occupy Palestine, it follows that the Palestinians have the "duty" to make room and give up their homeland. If the Palestinians refuse to give up their land, then the Palestinians are "guilty" of having failed to fulfill their duty. If the Palestinians are guilty, the Shaker Heights Jews have the right to enforce what is their right and force the guilty Palestinians out of their land.

Accordingly, the use of force by the Zionist Jews of America, Europe and elsewhere against the Palestinians is a legitimate right of the Jews, if one assumes that they have the right to occupy Palestine. This assumption is not only absurd, but it is also racist and implies the "right to commit aggression." In the Twentieth Century we cannot admit such a right and, therefore, we cannot admit the Zionist premise.

What if the Palestinians refuse to give up their homes to the Jews of Shaker Heights or the Jews of Kalamazoo? The best way to evict the Palestinians is to terrorize them by killing at random any number of women and children to frighten the rest to leave.

Hence terrorism is an essential element of Zionist doctrine. Indeed, the Zionists introduced terrorism to the Middle East and the Palestine conflict!

3. *Persecution*—It goes without saying that the atrocities committed against the Jews during the Twentieth Century were more terrible than those committed by the barbarians or by the primitive man. However, it should be recalled that Jewish persecution in Europe was the fault and responsibility of Nazi Germany, not the Arabs. The

Western sense of guilt for what happened to the Jews in the West and by Western hands cannot be relieved by helping the poor Jews to occupy the home of the poor Palestinians. Generosity to the Jews at the expense of innocent Arabs is morally reprehensible. The Arabs should not be expected to pay for the crimes of Hitler. Jewish persecution in Europe may vest the Jews with certain rights against Germany, but surely not against the Palestinians.

There are those who claim that the horror of the holocaust did not take place or that the number of the Jewish victims of those horrors was not 6 million human beings, but less.

Whether there was one innocent Jew victimized by the Nazis or 6 million or 10 million, all of it is evil. The Holy Quran condemns such acts in these words, "He who kills one innocent person is as if he has killed the whole mankind."

Accordingly, the universal condemnation of the Nazis for their crimes against the Jews, Poles, Gypsies, Russians and others should be permanent and with no reservation. But let it be made clear that whether the Nazis killed one Jew, 6 million or more, this does not entitle the Jews to occupy an inch of Palestine or kill a single Palestinian.

4. *Jewish "know-how"*—Also perpetuated in America is the argument regarding the Jewish "know-how." For in their attempt to support their general position, the Zionists refer to the Jewish ability to improve the land of Palestine and the Arab inability to do so! Whatever validity the claim regarding Jewish ability might have, it does not entitle the Jews to go to someone else's home, against his will, to "improve" that home.

Indeed, a Zionist Jew from Europe with a doctorate degree in soil chemistry should be able to improve the land. But if this argument is accepted, then the Communists with their technical know-how will be entitled, as a matter of right, to go to other countries, against the will of the people, to "improve" those countries. The Zionist argument is indeed reminiscent of Hitler's theory that Germany was entitled to occupy Poland because the Germans could improve Polish agriculture.

The ability of the European Jew to "improve" the land is not due to the fact that he is "Jewish," rather because he is "European" and a product of modern Western "know-how."

The talk that the Jews can teach the Arabs to develop their agriculture and industry is at best an insult to the Arabs. It would be an insult to the Americans if Russia with its superior knowledge of rockets and spaceships assumed the responsibility of teaching the Americans, regardless of America's wishes, how to make Sputnik and how to whisk a man around the world in a spaceship and establish and maintain space stations.

For human beings have intangible values which are even more important than economic, material and scientific progress. Just as the Poles would have preferred to improve their "backward" agriculture their own way, without Hitler's intrusion, and the Americans prefer advancing their space program without Russian imposed instruction, so do the Arabs, in their new awakening, obviously prefer carrying on their developing without Zionist intrusion.

The Zionists speak of having made paradise out of the desert and this appeals greatly to the Americans who think with their hearts. Of course, when billions of American dollars are poured yearly on a small piece of land, it should bring some changes and improvements to that land. The credit, at least in part, should go to America which has supplied the funds and to Western civilization which supplied the know-how. The Israelis and Zionists continually boast of the achievement, yet rarely give credit where it is due.

5. *Land "purchased"*—Another aspect of the question of Palestine is the issue of land purchase and the one-sided presentation in America that the Jews bought the land in Palestine. The Jews did indeed purchase *some* of the land and much was given to them as grant-in-aid by the British authorities. However, according to the *Survey of Palestine*, pp. 103 and 243, by 1920 the Jews owned 2.5 percent of the land. By 1945, they had bought and otherwise acquired legal title to 3.56 percent. This made the total of Jewish land ownership 6.06 percent. From 1945 to 1948 the Jews bought, according to the most generous estimates, less than 1 percent, making the total Jewish owned land by 1948 no more than 7 percent of Palestine. Considering the fact that nearly 13 percent of the land in Israel (under the partition plan) belonged to the 180,000 Arabs who were still there by 1948, it follows that some 80 percent of the land under Israeli control was acquired by sheer brutal force of occupation from its rightful owners, the Palestinian Arab people.

This point has been confirmed by the United Nations. According to the 1951 Progress Report of the United Nations Conciliation Commission for Palestine (A/1985), p. 16, the total Arab land passed to Israeli hands was 16,324 square kilometers. This is 80 percent of the total (20,850 square kilometers) land under Israeli control. The Zionist Jews took over the whole Arab cities of Jaffa, Acre, Lydda, Beit Shan, Magdal, Beersheba, in addition to 388 towns and villages and large parts of 94 others. In this process they confiscated over 10,000 shops, 120,000 dunums of orange groves, (4.05 dunums equals one acre), 40,000 dunums of vineyards and at least 10,000 dunums of other orchards and nearly 95 percent of the olive groves. None of this has been paid for. And very little of this is known in America.[11]

6. *"Feudalist" opposition*—Also circulated is the notion that the Arab feudalists and reactionary governments, fearful of a progressive Israel to challenge the feudal order, are opposing Israel, and that when feudalism is overthrown and the standard of living raised, the Arab people will be pleased with the blessings of Israel and will live in peace and amity with the Jewish state. The claim that Arab feudalism is the cause of the opposition to Israel is a charge belied by facts. To be sure, the feudalists oppose Israel. But this is no greater than the opposition to Zionism expressed by Arab farmers, businessmen, workers, students and so on.

The Arab intelligentsia, who know of their rights and refuse to be subjugated to humiliation and injustice, have opposed Zionism most vehemently and there is no doubt they will continue to oppose Zionist encroachment for many generations. The Zionists' assertion that Arab feudalists (most of them illiterate) instruct the educated Arabs (hundreds of thousands with university education) and direct them to oppose Zionism and Jewish intrusion in Palestine is plainly absurd and plainly ridiculous. Yet this absurd contention has had a wide circulation in America, thanks, once more, to those who influence American public opinions and do the thinking for the people who have no time to think with their heads.

7. *United Nations' Role*—The Zionists argue that the Arabs opposed and disregarded the 1947 United Nations Partition Plan which created Israel, and this is presented in America as a legal charge against the Arabs and the anti-Zionist world.

It requires little imagination to visualize the American reaction to a United Nations scheme to partition Alaska (even when it was a territory), giving a small portion thereof to a group of white Russians, to whom Alaska originally belonged, or to give a small portion of southern California to Mexico. Surely America would oppose such a plan and disregard it, if it did not take steps to expel U.N. Headquarters from the continent and withdraw from the organization.

The fact is that the United Nations is forbidden by its Charter (Article 2, paragraph 7) to intervene in matters which are essentially within the domestic jurisdiction of the states, much less to partition territories against the will of their inhabitants. Of course, the U.N. may make recommendations. But these recommendations are not binding unless ratified by those involved. Accordingly, the Partition Plan of 1947 was not binding at the time on the Palestinians or the Arabs.

At the present, however, a case could be made for the validity of that U.N. Plan on two grounds: first, that Israel and the Arab States signed, on May 12, 1949, the Laussane Protocol, in which they agreed to settle their dispute on the basis of the Partition Plan; and second, the repeated affirmation and reaffirmation by the United Nations, ever since 1947, of its Partition Plan Resolution.

The Zionists' reference to the United Nations would indeed bewilder the informed observer. Which United Nations do the Zionists talk about? Is it the United Nations whose resolution support the Zionists' arguments, or the United Nations whose resolutions the Zionists have disregarded for more than three decades? The Arab states have been insisting ever since 1949 that the United Nations Resolution should be implemented in order to establish peace in the Middle East; the Zionists, on the other hand, have consistently defied the said Resolution. Neither the Arab insistence on the implementation of U.N. resolutions nor their disregard by the Israelis have been brought to the attention of the American people, who do not know much about these vital issues and care less.

There are hundreds of occasions on which the United Nations has dealt with the Palestine problem and resolved accordingly. The substantive part of the majority of these resolutions deals with (1) the right of Palestine Arab refugees to return to their homes and those who refuse repatriation to be compensated by Israel; (2) internationalization of Jerusalem, and (3) establishment of permanent borders. But the American people know very little or nothing about these resolutions.

In this connection, the late Roger Baldwin, President Emeritus and founder of the American Civil Liberties Union, wrote in 1959:

It has long been obvious that the initiative for any settlement of the Arab refugee problem must come from Israel. The United Nations has held so for a decade, insisting that no solution is in sight unless the refugees are given the right to choose between repatriation and resettlement.[12]

8. & 9. *Responsibility for War and Flight of Refugees*—The Zionists also argue and have circulated the arguments that in 1948 the Arabs attacked Israel and that Palestinian Arabs left of their own accord.

To start from the events of 1948 and forget the events which led to that date assumes that history lives in a vacuum and that historical events are isolated from each other. This is inadmissible. The fact is that the first attack on Arab rights began when the Zionist Jews of Europe moved into Palestine at least as early as 1917. Zionist intrusion in Palestine with British help was the beginning of the attack on Arab rights.

The question may be raised concerning the chain of events and the reason why one should go back to 1917 and not 70 A.D. when the Jews were dispersed from Palestine. The reason for not returning 2,000 years is because of the fact that whatever happened to the Jews 2,000 years ago does not vest the Jews of today with any rights in Palestine (the most liberal statute of limitation expires in 15 years), and the fact that whatever happened to the Jews of 2,000 years ago was not the fault of the Palestine Arabs of today. But the Balfour Declaration of 1917 marks the beginning of formal Zionist and Western assaults on Palestine in recent years and, hence, the start of Zionist attacks on Arab rights.

When Dr. Chaim Weizmann, the Zionist leader and later the first President of Israel, was asked about his conception of the "national home" phrase of the Balfour Declaration, he said that the Zionists understood by the national home in Palestine a right to make Palestine "as Jewish as England is English."

If Palestine were to become as Jewish as England was English, then the 93 percent Arabs of Palestine, both Moslems and Christians, were condemned by the Zionists from the very beginning to become a minority in their own home. It was natural then that the Arabs of Palestine would resent the terms of the Balfour Declaration, and to them the British action was at best a reflection of pseudo-humanitarianism and over-generosity at the expense of the Arabs. And it was natural that the Arabs would resent becoming a minority in their home and against their own will. As the result of Arab resentment, violence erupted in Palestine in 1922, 1926, 1928, 1933 and 1936. The Zionists, having discovered the Arabs' refusal to

48

become a minority in their home, adopted a new slogan towards the Arabs, "The only good Arab is a dead Arab."

As it was impossible for the seven percent Jews of Palestine to become, even through Jewish immigration, a majority (especially in the light of the rapid natural increase of the Arab population), the Zionists had to resort to other means to make the Arab majority a minority. The means was terrorism and included the destruction of Arab villages and the wholesale murder of Arab men, children and women, creating fear amongst the Arab population and causing them to flee the land.

In his *Revolt*, Menachim Begin, the Jewish terrorist turned prime minister, declares that his attacks on the Arab towns and villages caused the great panic among Palestine Arabs, leading to their exodus. Indeed, many Arab villages fell to the Zionists—long before the so-called Arab attack on Israel on May 15, 1948.

The New York Times reports the fall of the following Arab villages and towns to the Zionist hands:

Gazaza (December 21, 1947), Sa'sa' (February 16, 1948), Haifa (February 21, 1948), Bir Adas (March 6, 1948), Deir Yaseen (April 10, 1948), Tiberias (April 20, 1948), Jerusalem (April 25, 1948), Jaffa (April 26, 1948), Acre (April 27, 1948), Safad (May 7, 1948), and so on until May 15.

The Zionists' attack, occupation and destruction of Arab villages and towns caused the flight of Palestine Arabs. Toynbee declares that the Zionist Jews "evicted" the Arabs of Palestine from their home. And Toynbee's observation is confirmed by no less an authority than David Ben Gurion. He writes in his *Rebirth and Destiny of Israel*, 1954, pp. 530–531:

Until the British left (May 15, 1948), no Jewish settlement, however remote, was entered or seized by the Arabs, while the Haganah. . .captured many Arab positions and liberated Tiberias and Haifa, Jaffa and Safad.

And, again pp. 291–292:

The Haganah did its job: until a day or two before the Arab invasion not a settlement was lost, no road cut, although movement was seriously dislocated despite express assurances of the British to keep the roads safe so long as they remained. Arabs started fleeing from the cities almost as soon as disturbances began in the early days of December (1947). As fighting spread, the exodus was joined by Beduin and fellaheen, but not the remotest Jewish homestead was abandoned, and nothing a tottering administration could unkindly do stopped us from reaching our goal on May 14, 1948, in a State made larger and Jewish by the Haganah.

The Zionists charge that Arab radios ordered Palestine Arabs to leave. After a thorough examination of the 1948 Arab press and the B.B.C.-monitored transcripts of broadcasts from Arab capitals and secret Arab radio stations, Prof. Walid Khalidi of the American University of Beirut concludes that the Palestine Arabs were urged and ordered by Arab leaders and governments *not* to leave Palestine. On the other hand, Zionist radios, dramatizing the massacre of Arab villagers in Deir Yaseen and elsewhere, warned that the same fate would befall other villagers if they did not evacuate within a definite time.

On the question of the Arab refugees and Zionist arguments, Erich Fromm writes:

> It is often said that the Arabs fled, that they left the country voluntarily, and that they therefore bear the responsibility for losing their property and their land. It is true that in history there are some instances—in Rome and in France during the revolution—when enemies of the state were proscribed and their property confiscated. But in general international law, the principle holds true that no citizen loses his property or his rights of citizenship; and the citizenship right is *de facto* a right to which the Arabs in Israel have much more legitimacy than the Jews. Just because the Arabs fled? Since when is that punishable by confiscation of property and by being barred from returning to the land on which a people's forefathers have lived for generations? Thus, the claim of the Jews to the land of Israel cannot be a realistic political claim. If all nations would suddenly claim territories in which their forefathers had lived two thousand years ago, this world would be a mad-house.

Dr. Fromm goes on to say:

> I believe that, politically speaking, there is only one solution for Israel, namely, the unilateral acknowledgment of the obligation of the State toward the Arabs—not to use it as a bargaining

point, but to acknowledge the complete moral obligation of the Israeli State to its former inhabitants of Palestine.[13]

The intrusion of the Zionist Jews into Palestine being an encroachment on Arab rights, the creation and expansion of the Israeli State was an act of injustice and aggression inflicted by brutal force upon the Arabs. Of course, the Arabs share part of the responsibility: their crime was in the fact that they were weak; if they were strong, they would have never permitted a single Zionist intruder to step ashore in Palestine. The fact that the Arabs were not strong led to the occupation of Palestine by the Zionist Jews and the displacement of the people of Palestine.

The Zionists talk about "seven Arab armies" attacking the infant, little Israel and the miraculous ability of some 650,000 Jews to defeat some 40 million Arabs. What the Zionists fail to compare is the actual fighting forces of the two parties. Syria and Lebanon had achieved their independence two years earlier in 1946. By 1948 their armies consisted of some 7,500 and 3,500 men, respectively. The corrupt regime of King Farouk in Egypt was able to mobilize 10,000 men and Iraq could count on 21,000 while Saudi Arabia was able to provide only two battalions. Jordan's Arab Legion consisted of 6,000 well-trained men who, however, lacked adequate ammunition. The total Arab force was at best around 47,500.

On the other hand, the Jews in Palestine had a mobilized, well-trained and equipped force of some 80,000 men consisting of the Haganah, Irgun and the Stern groups. The Jewish army had about 20,000 men with combat experience during World War II, and some 300 British-trained or British officers who were Zionist Jews and renounced their British citizenship at the last moment. Former "Israeli" Foreign Minister Abba Eban was one of them, with a South African passport.

Many American Jewish officers also renounced their American citizenship and placed their American training at the disposal of Israel. The case of Col. David (Mickey) Marcus is only one. Col. Marcus, who fell in action in 1948 while commanding the Jerusalem Front of the Israel army, was "a West Point graduate, one-time U.S. Attorney, Correction Commissioner of New York, World War II fighting officer, Presidential Advisor at many international conferences." He "left a thriving New York law practice to help organize the army of the new State of Israel in 1948."[14]

In addition to the well-equipped army, the Israelis had the financial and political support of the two mightiest powers on earth, America and Russia.

When these facts are taken into consideration, one will find that the "poor," "little," "tiny," "infant" Israel was powerful, strong and supported by strong powers. The Zionists' reference to "poor, little Israel" is only for the purpose of appealing to the emotions of good-hearted people who are unfamiliar with the facts and historical events, the people who think with their hearts. And the repeatedly one-sided presentation of the question of Palestine by the news media would deny the American people the opportunity of becoming acquainted with the facts, seeing the whole picture and thinking with their heads.

Today the Zionists and Israelis talk continuously about their desire for peace. This recalls the remarks of Von Clausewitz: "The aggressor is always a lover of peace; he would like to enter our homes unopposed." The Arabs' attitude toward these Israeli gestures is exactly like the American response to Japanese and German calls for peace in 1941.

10. *Refugee resettlement*—The Zionists have also perpetuated the notion that not only Palestinian refugees left their homes in Palestine of their own accord, but also that the Arab governments are holding the refugees as hostages in a game of political football, and have refused to resettle them. The argument that Arab leaders have refused to resettle the Palestinian refugees elsewhere in Arab land assumes that Palestine Arab refugees are inanimate objects who can be removed and resettled at the whim of Arab leaders. The Arab leaders have no right to decide on behalf of the refugees; it is the refugees themselves who have the right to decide regarding their own future. The decision of the Palestinian refugees has so far been that they want to return to their homes from which they were evicted by the Zionist Jews. In this decision the refugees have the moral and legal right with full backing of the United Nations which has recognized their right to return to their homes.

Regarding the suggestion that the refugees should be resettled elsewhere, Ambassador Henry Labouisse, former Director of United Nations Relief and Works Agency, said in 1958, that:

the refugees do not want to move further away. They want to return to their homes. The great majority do not even want to establish themselves as permanent residents of the countries in which they are now. They are afraid that by doing so, they might prejudice their rights to be eventually repatriated.[15]

If the refugees themselves refuse "to move further away," then the talk that Arab leaders do not resettle them elsewhere is a misrepresentation and an attempt to eliminate Israeli guilt and place the blame on the Arabs. The American attitude toward the question of the Palestinian refugees has been shaped by the Zionist presentation and viewpoint and in all fairness this is not a fair attitude nor is it based on the facts.

11. *"Bastion of Democracy"*—Then there is the widely circulated claim that Israel is a bastion of democracy in the midst of a sea of Arab dictatorship, and there is practically no American politician who has not repeated this phrase in his various speeches to the potential Jewish voters and donors.

As a "Jewish" state, Israel is a state which is based either on "religion" or "race" or an ethno-religious combination of some kind, similar to WASP. The concept of a Jewish state, Moslem state or Christian state belongs to the Middle Ages, not to the twentieth century. The Second World War was waged to defeat Fascism, the political philosophy of which was based on racism. Israel today seems to be based on a theory of the primacy of the Jewish "race" or "religion" and the claim to a chosen people status, whatever that means. Accordingly, Israel may be more accurately described as a "Bastion of Theocracy" in the Middle East, not a democracy.

To support their claim that Israel is a democracy, the Zionists point to the fact that there are some Arab representatives in the Israeli Parliament. What is not presented to the American people is the fact that most of these "Arabs" in the Israel Parliament were elected not by the Arabs in Israel, but by the Israeli Communist Party; hence they represent not the Arabs, but the Communists of Israel. Other "Arabs" in the Israeli Parliament are affiliated with the Jewish Labor Party and vote even against their own people if so directed by the Party. Then, of course, the fact is that the Arabs are more entitled to participate in any form of government in their land than the Jews who went to Palestine from Europe and America and who are, in the eyes of the non-Zionist world, intruders into Palestine.

Of course, due to their short modern history, the Arab states could hardly be expected to have meaningful democratic institutions. And democracy is more than the formalities of a parliament and elections, free or otherwise. On the all-important and crucial issue of equality of the people under the law and separation of religion from state, the trend in the Arab lands is toward these goals. The Jewish state of Israel, on the other hand, has relegated its non-Jewish, Arab minority to a position of second class citizenship. It has mixed religion and state in an unholy wedlock. Accordingly, the questions of personal status (marriage, divorce, etc.) are subject to religious, not civil, courts. Furthermore, the Israeli State builds synagogues (but not churches or mosques) and assigns rabbis and pays their salaries.

If there is any "democracy" in Israel, it is surely not for its Arab citizens who have been placed in the Jewish State in a position of permanent minority. Not even all the Jewish citizens of Israel enjoy equal rights. Since questions of personal status and religious performance by Jews have been entrusted to the Orthodox Jews, the position of the Reform and Conservative Jews in Israel is one of a discriminated minority. A Reform Rabbi is not permitted to officiate at a marriage, nor to conduct religious services as freely as the Orthodox Rabbis do. The truth is that American Jews enjoy a greater measure of religious freedom in America than they would enjoy in the Jewish State of Israel.

Israel can be described as a "Jewish democracy" and a "Jewish democracy" is a contradiction in terms. Israel can either be a "democracy" or "Jewish," but not both.

Assuming that in the "Jewish democracy" of Israel the number of Arabs, which in mid-1987 is about 35 percent of the total population, becomes 51 percent in a few years, would the Arab majority be permitted to form the government and change the name "Israel" into "Palestine"? Will there then be the "Jewish State of Palestine" or will it be the "Jewish State of Israel" with a 51 percent suppressed Arab majority?

Rabbi Meir Kahane admits that a "Jewish democracy" is a contradiction in terms. He would rather have a "Jewish State" than a "democracy" in which the Arabs have the peaceful possibility of becoming a majority. The rest of the Zionist Jews, seeing the ugly nature of this logical position, denounce Kahane and cling to the contradictory proposition. However, those who are against Kahane will sooner or later have to join Kahane. What will they do if the Arabs become 51 percent? Kahane is, therefore, more honest than other Zionists who are hypocrites. In the long run, however, all Zionists are Kahanes!

None of these various undemocratic features of Israel have been brought to the attention of the American people by the American press.

As for the Zionist argument that Israel is America's "trusted ally" suffice it to recall that Israel is "America's greatest charity," receiving some $15 million daily from the U.S. taxpayers. Yet the same Israel has created hatred against America and is the cause of violence in the Middle East against Americans and other Westerners. Furthermore, Israel, "the trusted ally," has spied on the United States, stolen American secrets and whenever it feels that its interests are not compatible with American interest, it has rebuked America and American politicians and presidents publicly.

To give all that money and support to win one supposedly "trusted" ally and alienate some twenty-two Arab and some forty-six Muslim countries is a poor bargain. The United States should stop its $15 million daily allowance to Israel and gain immediately the friendship and trust of some one billion people in the Arab and Muslim worlds. Senator Rudy Boschwitz and other Zionist apologists who claim that Israel is a "strategic asset" for America turn the facts upside-down. They consider the cause of American difficulties in the Middle East and the Muslim world as an asset. American support of this "asset" is the cause of terrorism against America!

12. *Arab "anti-Semitism" and discrimination against the Jews—* Another misrepresented conception is the cry that Saudi Arabia and other Arab states discriminate against American Jewish citizens. Here again the effect is presented as the cause. According to the Israeli "Law of Return" and "Nationality Law", American Jews, but not American Christians or members of other religions or racial backgrounds, are given the facilities to go to Israel and become automatically Israeli citizens.

This Israeli legislation is based on the Zionist doctrine that the Jews outside Palestine/Israel are residing in foreign lands, and according to the doctrine, the American Jews are Israelis residing in exile and are potential Israeli citizens. Because of this Israeli assumption and law (which has not been repudiated by American Zionist Jews, but has been tacitly approved by them through their actions on behalf of Israel which speak loudly of their consent to and approval of the Israeli assumption) the Arabs are forced to consider the so-called "American" Jews as potential Israelis and, therefore, potential enemies.

Briefly, Arab policy towards persons of Jewish background is not a policy motivated by anti-Semitism. It is a resentment of Zionist intrusion in Palestine based on *political* grounds and not on religious or racial bigotry or hatred.

The problem can also be viewed from a different angle. If the Arabs discriminate against "American Jews" it is because Israel discriminates against "American Christians." By conferring upon American Jews certain rights and privileges, Israel is discriminating against the rest of the American people. The Arabs are not barring or discriminating against *Americans* any more than are the Israelis; the Arabs are merely barring potential Israeli citizens and enemy aliens from entering Arab lands.

The American Zionist Jews cannot have it both ways. They accept special privileges from Israel, putting them above other Americans, and protest against disabilities which result from that privileged position. Only if the American Jews repudiate and denounce the Zionist assumption and Israeli laws which have conferred upon them special rights, can they logically protest against Arab legislation which gives special rights to the American Christians and others, and not to the Zionist Jews. Those American Jews who have objected to Zionist assertions have been welcomed in all Arab lands, like other Americans. This fact is not well known in this country either, because the news media has not been fair.

13. *Forgetting the past*—Then there is the constructive advice generously offered by the Zionist and circulated by the American press and politicians, "Let's forget about the past and start from here." This is a clear example of Zionist double-talk. For while the entire Zionist claim to Palestine was based upon historical grounds—namely, that Palestine belongs to the Jews because in the remote past of 3,000 years ago Hebrew tribes conquered Palestine and that the Jews have not forgotten Palestine over the past 2,000 years. They turn around and ask the Arabs to forget about their homes, in which they were born and raised and from which they were evicted only recently.

The Zionists argue that you cannot turn back the clock of history and permit Palestinian refugees to go to their homes. Alas! It was the Zionists who found in the 2,000-years-ago story a logical ground to turn the clock of history 2,000 years. There are, then, according to the Zionists, two standards for Zionist and Arab sentimental attachments, rights and behavior: the Zionists can turn back the clock of history 2,000 years, whereas the Arabs should not attempt to turn it back after a few decades.

The advice, "let's forget about the 'past'" means in reality that the Arabs should forget about their rights. This the Arabs will not do.

14. *Israel exists*—Finally there is the Zionist argument repeated continuously by American politicians and non-politicians that "Israel is there; it is a fact" and that the Arabs should recognize it. Of course, this argument ignores the grave moral issue created by the Zionists as a result of their intrusion into Palestine against the will of the Arabs, and the countless injustices done to the Palestinians and other Arabs in the process.

In Machiavellian terms, it means that "Israel is there by force" and must be accepted.

When an argument is based on force, it invites no further argument to settle the question; it invites instead another force. Indeed, the argument that "Israel is there" is a double-edged weapon. It implies that because it is *there*, no argument should be raised—and likewise when it is *not there*, no further argument is needed. It is because of this that arguments based on *fait accompli*, rather than on the merits and legitimacy of the case, are never conducive to reconciliation and peace; such an argument will be a defiance and, therefore, an invitation to force.

The tragedy, of course, is not that the Zionists have advanced such arguments. The tragedy is in the fact that such arguments have found a wide circulation in America, and the Americans are a people with a sense of fair play, reasonableness, pride and self-respect, who would never accept any of these arguments if they were advanced in a case against America. Yet the newspapers, the columnists, radio and television commentators, the politicians and the "objectivists" have all capitalized intentionally or unintentionally on American sympathies and good intentions, and thereby have misrepresented the Arab case and misled the American people. In the process they have smeared the once-wholesome American image in the Middle East and painted him as ugly as they could. The ugly Arab in the American press created the ugly American in the Middle East.

* * *

But why did the American Government and the West support

Zionism despite the fact that its moral position is at best dubious and its success resulted in the most unfortunate political repercussions for the West? There are several reasons for Western support of Zionism.

To begin with, there is a vague, unclear and hazy notion in the American and Western mind that somehow the Jews are a people apart, belonging to a different land. Of course, this notion has been strengthened by the Zionist attitude, behavior and ideology.

Hence the idea of "let the Jews go somewhere else and have their own country" does not appear, on the surface, to be strange or morally wrong. The Zionists, of course, profit by such an attitude.

The above general and vague notion receives further support from two groups, who, for different reasons, have helped Zionism at the expense of the people of Palestine. The first group is the anti-Semites, who in their attempt to "get rid of the Jews" lend their support to the Zionist slogan of "let the Jews go home."

The second group is the progressives and liberals, who have developed a sense of guilt for what happened to the Jews in the West and by Western hands. In their attempt to relieve their sense of guilt, they have been willing to help the poor Jews find homes and establish a state—provided, however, that the Jewish state shall be established not in Missouri or California, but in the far away land of Palestine. On this, the "liberals" would retort that the Jews have not demanded a state in Missouri or California. But assuming that there was such a Jewish demand, would Americans ever permit the creation of a *separate, sovereign Jewish state* in New York or anywhere in the United States?

If the answer is "no," then the conclusion is inevitable that these "liberals," who have been helping the poor European Jews in the home of the poor Palestinian Arabs, must be either ignorant of Arab rights and the absurdity of the Zionist "historical" claim, and hence misled, or the "liberal'" support of Zionism is the result of hidden anti-Semitism and a latent desire to "get rid of the Jews."

But whatever the motives, the anti-Semites and the so-called liberals and humanitarians have done the Palestine people a great wrong as the result of their direct or indirect, intentional or unintentional, support of Zionism.

Then there is another reason for the Western support of Zionism which has nothing to do with anti-Semitism or with humanitarianism, pseudo or otherwise. This third reason finds its origin in cold, calculated power politics.

President Truman refers, in his *Memoirs*, Vol. II, p. 158, to the mounting Jewish pressure on the White House to create a Jewish state in Palestine. He writes:

> I do not think I ever had as much pressure and propaganda aimed at the White House as I had in this instance. . .actuated by political motives and engaging in political threats. . .

Truman goes on to describe the subtle ways in which the Zionists affected American policy, pp. 160–161:

> As the pressure mounted, I found it necessary to give instructions that I did not want to be approached by any more spokesmen for the extreme Zionist cause. I was even so disturbed that I put off seeing Dr. Chaim Weizmann, who had returned to the United States and had asked for an interview with me. My old friend, Eddie Jacobson, called on me at the White House and urged me to receive Dr. Weizmann at the earliest possible moment. Eddie, who had been with me through the hard days of World War I, had never been a Zionist. In all my years in Washington he had never asked me for anything for himself. He was of the Jewish faith and was deeply moved by the sufferings of the Jewish people abroad. He had spoken to me on occasions, both before and after I became President, about some specific hardship cases that he happened to know about, but he did this rarely. On March 13 he called at the White House.

President Truman could be forgiven for being "so disturbed" that he put off seeing Dr. Weizmann. But his statement that Eddie "had never been a Zionist" is most disturbing. After all, it was Mr. Jacobson, the "non-Zionist," who succeeded in the service of Zionism when old time Zionists failed. Truman goes on:

> I was always glad to see Eddie. Not only had we shared so much in the past, but I have always had the warmest feelings toward him. It would be hard to find a truer friend. Eddie said that he wanted to talk about Palestine. I told him that I would rather he did not and that I wanted to let the matter run its course in the United Nations. . .
> Eddie was becoming self-conscious, but he kept on talking.

He asked me to bear in mind that some of the pro-Zionists who had approached me were only individuals and did not speak for any responsible leadership.

I told him that I respected Dr. Weizmann, but if I saw him, it would only result in more wrong interpretations.

One wonders as to how many Arab Americans had an open access to the White House, requesting the American President to listen to the views of Arab leaders.

Truman goes on to describe the little skit played by Eddie, the rehearsal of which might have been conducted under the direction of some top Hollywood producers:

> Eddie waved toward a small replica of an Andrew Jackson statue that was in my office.
>
> He's been your hero all your life, hasn't he?" he said. "You've probably read every book there is on Andrew Jackson. I remember when we had the store that you were always reading books and pamphlets, and a lot of them were about Jackson. You put this statue in front of the Jackson County Court House in Kansas City when you built it."
>
> I did not know what he was leading up to, but he went on: "I have never met the man who has been my hero all my life," he continued. "But I have studied his past as you have studied Jackson's. He is the greatest Jew alive, perhaps the greatest Jew who ever lived. You yourself have told me that he is a great statesman and a fine gentleman. I am talking about Dr. Chaim Weizmann. He is an old man and a very sick man. He has traveled thousands of miles to see you and now you are putting off seeing him. That isn't like you."
>
> When Eddie left I left instructions to have Dr. Weizmann come to the White House as soon as it could be arranged. However, my visit was to be entirely off the record. Dr. Weizmann, by my specific instructions, was to be brought in through the East Gate. There was to be no press coverage of his visit and no public announcements.

The fact that Truman was unwilling to see more Zionist leaders and the fact that Eddie Jacobson was able to get Weizmann to Truman via Andrew Jackson are indicative of the Zionist pressure on the highest elected office in the land. Furthermore, it is indicative, as well, of the ways and means applied by the Zionists to achieve their aims.

Truman's "specific instructions" that Weizmann be brought to the White House through "the East Gate" and "without press coverage" and "announcements" is of little comfort to the Arabs and the non-Zionist world, as it is an admission on the part of the President of the United States of America that the morality of his action was less than honorable. But whether honorable or otherwise, the head of the Zionist movement found himself in the Office of the American President, and before him there was a stream of Zionists and Zionist sympathizers who advised the President of the United States and shaped American policy in the Middle East in Zionist and Israeli interests.

The Zionists enjoy power and exercise their influence through their wealth, contacts, ownership of some communication media or stock holdings, participation in these media, advertisements in the press and threat of withdrawal of advertising, sponsorship of radio and TV programs and threat of withdrawal of such sponsorship, their concentration in the strategic states which can make or unmake an election, and their creation of the myth of the "Jewish vote" to which every politician succumbs.

In addition to these factors, Zionist influence is exercised through the technique of blackmail and smear, accusing those who disagree with Zionism of anti-Semitism. By using the unsavory device of equating anti-Zionism with anti-Semitism, they employ a most vicious weapon of character assassination.

The Zionists' long list of "anti-Semites" includes all the Arabs, who are possibly more Semites than most Jews, including Sharon, Peres, Begin, Goldberg, Kahane and David Ben Gurion and Chaim Weizmann himself. Others who have been smeared by the Zionists as "anti-Semites" include such non-Zionists as Rabbi Elmer Berger, Dwight McDonald, David Riesman, Morris S. Lazaron, Roger Baldwin, Erich Fromm, William Zuckermann, Alfred M. Lilienthal and such persons with a long-standing record of fighting against Fascism and anti-Semitism as Dorothy Thompson, Arnold Toynbee, Richard H. Grossman and others who have dared to criticize Zionism.

While it is fashionable for Western liberals, primarily due to their sense of guilt for the crimes committed against the Jews, to be pro-Zionist, the support given to Zionism by some of the conservative elements must be analyzed in different terms. These "conservatives," many of whom are closely identified with reactionary groups in much of their outmoded economic thinking and international outlook, lean backward and support Zionism for good or no good reason, lest they should be labelled as anti-Semites.

Indeed, many "liberals" refrain from criticizing Zionism in order to avoid the charge of anti-Semitism. It is most likely that these elements are, consciously or unconsciously, anti-Semites at heart and, therefore, particularly desirous not to be labelled as anti-Semites. It takes a truly non-anti-Semite and a truly courageous person to criticize Zionism without the fear of the charges of anti-Semitism and the cries of "prejudice."

In contrast to the Zionist power and influence on the liberals and conservatives, experts and politicians, the Arabs have neither the facilities nor the possibilities and proper circumstances to present their case to the American people and the American policy makers. Indeed, President Truman, who listened to the views of Zionist Chaim Weizmann, did not even heed the advice of his own Joint Chiefs of Staff and Cabinet members.

After referring to the fact that Secretary of the Navy James Forrestal and the Joint Chiefs of Staff had advised against his Palestine policy in 1947, President Truman goes on to admit that "The Department of State's specialists on the Near East were, almost without exception, unfriendly to the idea of a Jewish State." *Memoirs*, Vol. II. p. 162.

In 1947 and 1948, Secretary Forrestal attempted to decrease Zionist pressure on the United States Government by his endeavors to secure the agreement of the Democratic and Republic party leaders to keep the question of Palestine outside the field of domestic politics. His efforts were in vain because in the opinion of the Democratic Party politicians, "the Democratic Party would be bound to lose and the Republicans gain by such an agreement" and the Republican politicians feared that the Republicans might lose. In indignation, Forrestal remarked, "I think it is about time that somebody should pay some consideration to whether we might not lose the United States."

In a study published by the United States Senate Committee on Foreign Relations entitled *Summary of Views of Retired Foreign Service Officers*, the whole issue is put in a nutshell:

The crux of the problem was summed up by President Truman when he said, "I am sorry, gentlemen, but I have to answer hundreds of thousands who are anxious for the success of Zionism; I do not have hundreds of thousands of Arabs among my constituents."

It is significant to note that in giving their views regarding American policy in Western Europe, the Far East, Latin America and elsewhere, the American foreign service men disagreed as to the proper diagnosis of American policy in those regions. However, with regard to the Middle East, the American diplomats were *unanimous* that the creation of Israel with American support was the cause of American difficulties in the Middle East, and the greatest factor in creating the ugly American and causing violence and terrorism against Americans.

The whole creation of Israel was a mistake. One diplomat puts forth his views as follows:

It was an error for us to support in any way the establishment of an independent Jewish state in Palestine. . .it should be a firm policy of our Government to oppose its further expansion.

Another diplomat provides an analogy:

If a man goes to a doctor and is told that he has an incipient cancer that can almost certainly be eradicated by an operation and he then goes home and, although his condition deteriorates from year to year, does nothing about it, the time will eventually come when nothing can be done to save him. I fear that that is the history of our policy in the Near East.

The diplomat continues:

The foundation of Israel in an Arab country and our subsequent military, financial and political support of that state is an outstanding example of the way in which in a democracy the interests of our country are, and perhaps must be, sacrificed to the interests, or supposed interests, of a determined minority. . . The Arabs, who until the establishment of Israel had considered the United States the one foreign power on which they could rely and who had in Americans a confidence which they could give to no other foreigner, became alienated by what they considered our breach of faith.

Another diplomat writes indignantly:

There is probably no area where our foreign policy has been more criticized as vague, vacillating and ineffective than in the Middle East. Various reasons have been offered to explain the serious setbacks suffered by the Western Powers in that area, but the real underlying cause that got us off to such a bad start shortly after the conclusion of World War II is seldom mentioned, publicly at least. I refer to the creation, largely with the support of Great Britain and the United States, of the State of Israel. It certainly did not require a Talleyrand to foresee the trouble and bitterness which this act was bound to create in our relations with the Arab and Moslem worlds. . .

He goes on to say:

However, all that is now presumably water over the dam (not Aswan, of course) and probably the action was bound to come sooner or later; although one would hope, done with more consideration for Arab feelings and the thousands of Arab refugees that it left to seek asylum somewhere outside the borders of their own country. But to take an ostrich-head-in-the-sand attitude, as most people seem to do today, preferring not to know what was really responsible for our having lost, almost overnight, the friendship and respect of the Arab countries which, up to that time, had looked to us as the one disinterested country on whose support they could count is, in my opinion, both stupid and hypocritical.[16]

Thus, according to the testimony of the best informed authorities, the creation of Israel with American support under the pressure of the Zionists, is at the root of American difficulties in the Middle East. The minority of the Zionist Jews in America have been able, through well-organized and well-financed campaigns and drives, to direct the American policy toward the Middle East in support of Zionism and to the detriment of American prestige in the Arab and Muslim lands.

The American policy in the Middle East has been an ostrich's policy, stupid and hypocritical, due to the fact that the Zionists have been able to direct the herd and the herd has been willing to follow. The Zionist Jews have been able to put the pressure on the American politicians, and thence on the U.S. Government, because the majority of the American people have been either *uninformed or politically apathetic*, leaving the door wide open for the politically active minority of Zionists to determine the fate of the majority and U.S. policy in the Middle East.

By now many a reader who has been patiently skimming through these pages is inquiring impatiently, "Now, then, what is the answer? whatever the rights or the wrongs—what to do about it now? What is the solution?"

Of course it is natural that this question should be raised, particularly by the American people who are interested in peace and prosperity and whose pragmatic society has solved many problems, overcome many difficulties and provided answers to numerous questions. But surely one cannot know the "solution" to the question of Palestine, or any other issue, without knowing what the problem is in the first place.

To know the problem, let's put the shoe on the other foot. If the Americans can accept the establishment of a separate sovereign Jewish state in the wasteland of California or New York or Truman's Missouri against their will, assuming that the Jews originally came from California; that the Jews were persecuted in Germany and elsewhere; that the Jews can make paradise out of the deserts of California; that the United Nations had decided to give California, or a part thereof, to the Jews; that the Jews have the highest democratic society and that they can help and teach the Americans—if the Americans can ever accept these arguments, then they should expect the Arabs to accept the same.

Hence, any concession or reconciliation made by the Arabs to accept the Jews in Palestine will be generous and magnanimous indeed. The Arabs should not be expected to do what the Americans would refuse to do. Accordingly, any "solution" based on "forcing" the Arabs to accept Israel, as the politicians promise Zionist conventions, would only aggravate the situation and make Americans a greater target of Arab resentment, violence and terrorism. If the Arabs have been mistreated, then the first step toward alleviating the injustice is to recognize Arab rights and appreciate the Arab feeling and position.

But what is the solution? An answer will be presented in the following chapter.

Solution

The question invariably is raised, "What is the solution to the Israeli-Palestinian conflict?" Whatever the rights and whatever the wrongs of the past, we have to find a way out of the present dilemma which endangers world peace.

It is imperative to understand the basic issues as the first step in proposing the solution.

The Zionists claim that the Jews have the right to occupy Palestine because Hebrew tribes had occupied that land several thousand years ago. The Bible describes the conquest of Jericho as follows:

> "And they utterly destroyed all that was in the city, both man and woman, young and old, ox and sheep and donkey, with the edge of the sword.
>
> But Joshua had said to the two men who had spied out the country, "Go into the harlot's house, and from there bring out the woman and all that she has, as you swore to her."
>
> And the young men who had been spies went in and brought out Rahab, her father, her mother, her brothers, and all that she had. So they brought out all her relatives and left them outside the camp of Israel.
>
> But they burned the city and all that was in it with fire. Only the silver and gold, and the vessels of bronze and iron, they put into the treasury of the house of the Lord.
>
> And Joshua spared Rahab the harlot, her father's household, and all that she had. So she dwells in Israel to this day, because she hid the messengers whom Joshua sent to spy out Jericho."

JOSHUA, Chapter 6, Verses 21–25.

The brutality of the Hebrew tribes in capturing an destroying Jericho, killing "both man and woman, young and old, ox and sheep and donkey, with the edge of the sword" should make every humanist ashamed of those brutes. It was the first recorded case of genocide, committed in the name of God! Not only should people be ashamed of that act, but for the Zionists to claim a right based on those horrors is unbelievable. It is as if the Nazis, who committed the crime of genocide against the Jews, claim certain privileged positions because of their inhumanity and crimes.

The Jews of the world today, having been the intended victims of genocide, should dissociate themselves from the brutal behavior of the ancient Hebrew tribes, not claim a certain "right" as the result of that act of genocide. To blame that brutality on God was a wicked device to justify their action. God is never brutal; it was the brutality of the primitive tribes, attributed to the concept of God.

The Jewish soul, expressed by Jewish intellectuals and humanists, should be dissociated from those horrors. That will be a first step toward peace in the Middle East and is the challenge to the Jewish soul.

There are at least three broad solutions proposed for Mideast peace. First, and this is the essence of the Camp David Accord, is that the Arabs should recognize Israel with its full occupation of all of Palestine. Israelis would give the Palestinians some measure of self-rule in the 1967—occupied portions of Palestine, but retain sovereignty and with that, the foreign relations of the country.

Under this solution, the Israelis maintain, some publicly, some in subtle ways, that the Palestinians should go and establish their "Palestine state" in Amman, Jordan. The Zionists have been pushing the theory that "Jordan is Palestine" in preparation for the establishment of the Palestinian state in Jordan.

That will fulfill the goal of the Zionists as it will establish the Jewish state in Palestine. However this Jewish state will have no peace and, therefore, it will not provide security for the Jews, nor solve the Jewish question. Indeed the Jewish state has created an Arab question.

The second solution calls for the return of the Jews to their countries of origin or their immigration completely to North America, South America, western Europe, Australia and elsewhere. Those who advocate this solution invoke the Hebraic principle of "an eye for an eye." The Jews came from these lands, so it is only just to return to the countries from which they came or to countries that have been supportive in helping them to go to Palestine.

This solution will bring a great deal of hardship, in addition to the moral question of the right of the Jews who were born in Palestine. Assuming that their parents, who went to Palestine against the will of the Palestinians, had violated the human rights of the Palestinians, what is the fault of the children who were born on that land? Of course the children who were born on that land are benefiting from the violation of Palestinian rights by their parents. And so they are enjoying the fruit of aggression and if they wish to enjoy that fruit, at least they have the moral obligation to apologize to the Palestinians for the sins of their parents. This viewpoint is advocated by extreme Arab fringe organizations and does not enjoy general Arab support.

The third solution advocates a two-state system. This revolves around Resolution 242 of the Security Council of the United Nations of 1967. Broadly, that resolution calls for the recognition by the Arabs of the State of Israel, as had existed prior to June of that year, and the return of the West Bank and Gaza to Arab sovereignty (as if the occupation of Palestine from 1948 to 1967 had legitimized Jewish occupation of western portion of Palestine). Because the Jews had not occupied the eastern portion from Jerusalem to the river Jordan during this time, they had no right to its occupation and annexation.

Under this solution, there would be two states in Palestine, one with a capitol in Tel Aviv, say, and the other capital in Nablus, assuming the question of Jerusalem is resolved.

The two-state system does not solve the problem and will not bring peace to Palestine. It has to be noted that human rights refer to a specific relationship between the individual and a specific thing. A Palestinian who has a house in Haifa has his right to that house and not to a house in Nablus or Amman or Baghdad or Casablanca. Consequently, if he is denied the right to return to his house in Haifa, he is denied his human rights.

To say that a person of Palestinian origin has returned to his house in Nablas would not satisfy the human rights of the person from Haifa. If the Haifawi Palestinian is denied his right to his land, he will not be satisfied because some other Palestinian has regained his right to some other property in some other portion of Palestine. The Haifawi Palestinian will do his best, peacefully first, to return to his house in Haifa, or forcefully if he is denied the right to return to his home. Hence, violence will erupt in Haifa, Safad, Accre, Jaffa, Bersheba and western Palestine which was occupied by Israel in 1948 and which under this plan is to be recognized as the Jewish state in Palestine. Jewish occupation of western Palestine from 1948 to 1967 does not legitimize their occupation of that land and a state cannot be established on that illegitimate occupation. At least the legitimacy of such a state will never be recognized by the victims of its establishment.

The previous solutions, having been advocated for many years by various partisans, have failed so far to bring peace to the area.

Here is a new alternative. It starts from the assumption that the Jews have *no right* whatsoever to occupy Palestine on the absurd ground that some 3,000 years ago some Hebrew tribes captured that land from the Canaanites. But the Jews who do not have the right to occupy Palestine do, indeed, have a human *need* for Palestine as a result of the atrocities committed against them over the centuries. This human need of the Jews should be recognized. But, of course, the human right of the Palestinians to their land must be recognized in the first place.

Therefore, a solution which would recognize the *human need of the Jews and the human right of the Palestinians* to Palestine might lead to peace and justice for all. Accordingly, all Palestine should be for all Palestinians, including all the Jews. The Jews of America and Russia who wish to go to Palestine should be encouraged and assisted. But of course all the Palestinians who wish to return should be permitted to do so.

There should be one government in Palestine, ruled by political majority in the best spirit of democracy. There should be no Jewish state, nor Christian state, nor Muslim state in Palestine. The political majority may wish to vote for a Labor Party or a Progressive Party or a Republican Party or a Democratic Party. Whatever political party they may wish to choose, it should rule the country for a limited period of four years or five years, according to the constitution which will have to be adopted.

In order to satisfy the Jewish human need for an Israel, the new country shall have two names. It shall be called "Israel" to satisfy the Jewish human need, and it shall be named "Palestine" to satisfy the Palestinian human rights. Both are honorable names with equal historic significance to satisfy the human needs and right of the people who are in Palestine.

Jerusalem is sacred to one billion Muslims, one billion Christians and 15 million Jews. Under the alternative proposed here, Jerusalem will belong to all the monotheistic religions, rather than being under Jewish control.

Will the Palestinians and the Jews be able to live together? Of course, there will be many difficulties and many problems. The extreme Zionists, who are in the main pessimists afraid of change, will cry immediately that there will be another holocaust against the Jews and that the Jews will be massacred.

To allay these fears, international guarantees through the United Nations or bilateral agreements can be arranged to prevent any such violence by either party against the other. While in the recent years there have been more Jewish massacres of the Arabs from Deir Yassin to Sabra and Shatila, in the olden days the relationship between the Jews and the Arabs was one of amity. Indeed, advocates of peace remember the days of good relations between the Jews and the Muslims. They recall the fact that the height of the Jewish contribution to humanity was with the Arabs in Spain and that the return of that golden age should be the goal of everyone in Palestine.

They recall further that there have been hundreds of thousands of Protestants who have killed hundreds of thousands of Catholics, and hundreds of thousands of Catholics who have killed hundreds of thousands of Protestants during the 30 Years War and the Hundred Years War. And yet today Protestants and Catholics live peacefully in Europe and America. The question of Northern Ireland is political and is the exception.

Moreover, Americans were killing Germans and Japanese, and Germans and Japanese were killing Americans. But at this stage all that hatred of the past has been eliminated and an era of friendship and trade is linking the Americans to their former enemies. The same can happen in Palestine.

The advocates of this alternative also suggest that presently the Arabs spend about $5 billion yearly for military defense. On the other hand, America gives to Israel some $5 billion a year in military aid. When peace comes to the area, and Palestine has reverted to all the Palestinians, Arabs and Jews, that $10 billion a year could be spent on psychologists, psychiatrists, social workers, therapists and economists and others who can soothe the feelings, eliminate the fear and the apprehension of the Jews, and the Palestinian sense that they had been wronged by the West and by the Zionists. When the fears and the sense of injustice are removed, the road to meaningful peace in the interest of all the citizens of the new state will be paved.

The new state should have two names: It can be called "Palestine/

Israel" or "Israel/Palestine" or "Pal-Is" or "Is-Pal", on the pattern of Czecho-slova-kia and Yugo-slavia.

People who are concerned about peace and justice in Palestine/Israel should examine these thoughts and promote this new alternative. This alternative assumes the Jewish people are more important than the Jewish state. And in the interest of peace for the Jewish people, the exclusivist undemocratic Jewish "state" may have to wither into a broader Palestine/Israel arrangement than standing alone as a threat to peace and to the Jewish people.

Under this alternative, all the Palestinians should be permitted to return to Palestine over three or five year period and settle in their former homes or nearby in comparable homes. Also all the Jews (including American and Soviet Jews) should be permitted to go to Palestine. There should be free flow of people, Palestinians and Jews, to and from Palestine/Israel.

Some American Zionist Jews may argue against this alternative on the ground that the Arab birth-rate is high and within a few years the Arabs will become the majority in Pal/Is. If the Zionist Jews wish to retain a Jewish majority and fear that Arab high birth-rate will change that majority, they (American Zionist Jews) should immigrate, at least one or two million of them, to Is/Pal and in a peaceful, normal and natural way maintain the Jewish majority they desire!

The American Zionists cannot stay in America and demand an abnormal situation of permanent Jewish majority in the Palestine/Israel area.

The solution of the Palestine problem will end the major cause of terrorism against America in the Middle East.

71

Conclusion

"America stands tall," says President Reagan. But "it runs scared," says the evidence. American embassies all over the world are fortresses surrounded by "flower pots." Everyone knows that those are to protect the embassy from attack by so-called terrorists rather than for decoration. In many places, such as Beirut and the Gulf areas, the embassies are also protected by tanks and armed personnel. The traditional Marine guards who received the visitors and added color to the embassy have become larger in number and form a protective police force surrounding the U.S. compounds. Does America stand tall?

An American observer of the Middle East scene said once that prior to the U.S. recognition of Israel in 1948 an American flag on the car of an American embassy in the streets of the Arab world and the Muslim lands was as if it represented a letter of recommendation from Prophet Mohammad. After 1948, an American embassy car or a flag was a good target for the mobs to hit, he added. In the past America was protected by the love of the people of the Middle East. Presently it is hatred by the people and American embassies must be protected by tanks!

Why?

Look at American policy abroad! The United States has been supporting the wrong horse almost everywhere. The little kings and dictatorial presidents who have suppressed their own people and have claimed to be pro-American are "good boys" who deserve American support and have, indeed, received American backing. As a result, America has supported those rulers and kept them in power, but has lost the respect of the people of those lands. The rulers come and go, but the people stay. What a high price to pay for America to keep a few "yes men" in power around the world.

The Americans should brace themselves for further acts of terrorism. In the imperfect world, U.S. foreign policy brings the violent reaction of others, and American individuals will be the victims, just as people in other countries are victims of American foreign policy.

And so to prevent terrorism against Americans, American foreign policy may have to be re-examined by the American people. The people in a democracy cannot and should not vote every two or four years, entrusting their future to the hands of politicians whose first commitment is not the good of the people, but the good of the politician and his re-election.

Americans should recognize that the politician is willing to sell the moon to get votes. Hence, the unwholesome role of the pressure groups on domestic and foreign policy at the expense of the general good of the people. Naturally, in a democracy there has to be an important role for pressure groups. Pressure groups are as essential to democracy as the secret ballot. But if some pressure groups are concerned with their narrow interests and the majority of the people are apathetic and unaware of their own broader rights, that smaller group will railroad through its interests at the expense of the majority.

The end result is the strange foreign policy which is well-intentioned but almost everywhere is hated and despised. If the U.S. supports "A" to take the land of "B", the Americans should not be astonished if Victim-B tries to retaliate against America and Americans one way or another. If the Americans feel that it was justifiable to help "A" to take over the land of "B", then they should not be irked at the reaction of "B" and should not find "B's" action as strange, abhorrent or irrational. America is not the policeman of the world, nor has it been entrusted with the wisdom to do the proper thing on the international scene. Its judgments are not accepted by other nations and those nations who cannot fight back against the "wrong" judgment of the U.S.A. will try to retaliate against private American citizens, members of the U.S. community.

In addition to this kind of retaliation-terrorism based on some political ideology, there are the non-ideological terrorists. In the United States there have been so many incidents of mass killing in Texas, San Diego, Oklahoma and elsewhere. Such acts of "terrorism," carried out by persons who go berserk, are part of twentieth-century life as much as car accidents and industrial accidents. While it is difficult to provide any remedy for such emotional eruptions by mass killers and psychotics, a remedy can be found for those who engage in terrorism due to ideological reasons. We have to know the cause of their terrorism and provide the remedy.

It was suggested in the previous chapter that an alternative solution might bring peace and justice to the Middle East. The road toward that remedy starts in the streets of America through Washington, D.C. and to Palestine. The American people should oppose the U.S. government's arms aid and sale to the Middle Eastern coun-

73

tries. The United States gives some $15 million in aid to Israel every day and some $5 million to the Arab countries daily. Almost all that aid is military and should be stopped. The parties to the Mideast conflict will then have to solve their problems through pacific means. America has been the cause of war and, as the merchant of death in the Middle East, has unconscionably sold arms to the two sides. An enlightened American public opinion will be essential to the establishment of peace in the Holy Land. The first step is to stop the arms aid and arms sale to the Middle East. An international arms embargo should be imposed on the region.

Because terrorism is an unconventional warfare, to use conventional force against it will bring greater casualties and sacrifices. The American attack on Tripoli and Benghazi was costly to America and to Libya, and it did not stop terrorism. Likewise, the Israeli aggression in Lebanon in June 1982 in order, supposedly, to stop terrorism, has been a costly experience for Israel and has not stopped Palestinian rockets and Palestinian efforts to cross the border and return to their homes.

In the Middle East, Palestinian homelessness is the cause of Palestinian terrorism. Palestinians engage in hijacking because their whole country of Palestine has been hijacked by the Zionists, with the support of the west and America in particular. To provide a remedy for Palestinian homelessness should be the first task of the American people and government, as they were responsible, at least in part, for that homelessness. Likewise Lebanese terrorism against America is an extension of Palestinian homelessness.

The question has been raised whether Middle East terrorism will come to America as it has swept France and Italy before. The answer really depends on the United States' foreign policy. If you go there to kill them, they will come here to kill you.

This again calls for the re-evaluation of American foreign policy. If Americans find it justifiable to help Israeli terrorists to kill the people there, then they should not be astonished if they get killed here by some Middle Eastern terrorists.[17] They should face it with stoic dignity, with no complaint and no crying. If, on the other hand, they find no reason to help Zionist Jews to occupy Arab land and kill Arab people, then they should pressure the politicians to stop helping Israel militarily and stop selling arms to the Arabs.

To stop terrorism against America demands, briefly, for the Americans to think with their heads, not with their hearts.

74

Epilogue

Hostages and Captors: Victims of Terrorism and War

In December 1986 and again in February 1987, the author and a delegation from the National Council on Islamic Affairs, which included Arab-American Muslim activist Dale Shaheen, visited Beirut and Damascus, seeking the release of the hostages who were held by "Islamic" Jihad and other "Muslim" organizations.

When, in November 1986, the news broke out that the U.S. had attempted to give arms to Iran in order to free the hostages in Lebanon and that the representative of the Anglican Church, Terry Waite, was somehow linked to that plan, the American Muslim leaders felt that the credibility of Terry Waite had been destroyed and that it was the obligation of the American Muslims and Arabs to try their hand at securing the freedom of the hostages in Lebanon, particularly as the hostage holders claimed to be "Islamic" groups.

But how does one reach the hostages if no one knows who the hostage holders are, or their whereabouts? The only means available was to reach the hostage holders through the public news media. The American delegation appealed in press conferences in Beirut and Damascus to the hostage holders, in the name of Islam and humanity, to release the hostages and, at least as a first step, to contact the delegation. The delegation's first goal was to understand the causes that had led the hostage holders to do their terrible deed.

Press conferences followed press conferences and appeals followed appeals. In the meantime, the delegation met with religious leaders, including Sheikh Mohammad Mehdi Shamsuddin and Mohammad Hussein Fadhlallah in Beirut and Ahmad Koftaro in Damascus. Furthermore, in Beirut the delegation met with the Prime Minister, the Ministers of Education and Foreign Affairs, the Speaker of the House and other leading personalities of Lebanon. In Damascus, the delegation met with the President, Vice President, Foreign Minister and Minister of Information. None of these in

Beirut or Damascus were able to lead the delegation toward the captors. Indeed, the leaders did not know anything about them and, of course, had no authority over them.

The delegation was received by the Syrian and Lebanese officials with all courtesies and with regrets over their inability to direct the delegation toward the hostage holders. But the real importance of these meetings was in holding press conferences after each meeting and appealing to the hostage holders to contact the delegation.

And then one night, December 6, 1986, at 11 p.m., someone knocked at the door of the author's room in the Damascus Sheraton Hotel. The author opened the door, the man introduced himself and was welcomed in. The visitor was young bearded, handsome and from his accent it was clear that he was Lebanese. There was an hour and a half of discussion with the man, who, it gradually became evident, was the spokesperson for the hostage holders. It was an awkward meeting. Each party was trying to understand the thinking of the other party, exchanging some Arab hyperbole as they gauged each other's standing and credibility.

The spokesman for the hostage holders, to be called here "Y", was polite, articulate and exceptionally bitter. Suspicious and paranoid as he seemed to be, he was at the same time very confident in himself, dogmatic in his belief and authoritative in his remarks.

"Why are you holding these hostages?" the author asked "Y". "These hostages are innocent persons and have done no wrong. In the name of Islam, we appeal to you to release them," the author begged "Y". "We have come here to listen to your views and share with you our apprehension that the holding of the hostages is not in the interest of Islam nor the American Muslims nor the one billion Muslim people of the world. Why are you holding these hostages and why don't you release them?" the author asked.

After a lengthy silence, "Y" spoke in terse language and in an accusative tone.

He explained, "The entire family of the hostage holder 'terrorist' who has captured Terry Anderson of Associated Press—his entire family was wiped out by an American bomb."

"And the children of the hostage holder 'terrorist' captor of Joseph Cicippio were burned by American napalm, dropped over them by an American airplane piloted either by an American or a Russian or a Polish Jew."

He said, "The survivor of a Lebanese village, which had been

76

totally destroyed by the shells of the USS New Jersey, was responsible for capturing other American hostages."

"And so," he said, "who is the terrorist? Your government, which has supported Israel to kill some 20,000 Lebanese and Palestinians and wounding some 30,000 of us and destroying one-third of southern Lebanon? Or the hostage holders who have captured a few individuals, limited their freedom of movement and contact with the outside world, and yet feeding them and taking care of them as much as possible? The American government was the greatest terrorist in the world," he said, "notwithstanding the fact that America kills in a 'civilized' way, dropping its bombs by the most sophisticated airplanes, and notwithstanding that those decisions are made in a democratic way by the majority of the people and the decision to give those airplanes to Israel are also made by Congress in a democratic fashion," he said sarcastically.

The author pleaded with the spokesman for the captors that, in the name of Islam, we have to examine the full picture. Under Islam, the Quran states, "If some people have done you injustice, you should not inflict injustice on a third party. You should be just." He continued, "you may have legitimate complaints against the U.S. government and its policies, but what is the fault of the people you have captured? Terry Anderson is an innocent man!"

"And so was the grandmother of his captor. She was an innocent woman, yet American bombs killed her and her entire family!" the hostage holders' representative said.

The spokesman for the hostage holders complained again and again bitterly that America engaged in a double-standard policy. "The Americans talk about human rights in Russia and what they really mean is the right of the Soviet Jews to go to Israel," he said. They have no human concern for "the human right of the people of Palestine to return to their land of Palestine." The Americans want, in the name of human rights, to get the Jews out of Russia and settle them in the home of the Palestinians. How decent of them, those Americans concerned with human rights! He said.

And again and again he complained that America has killed 20,000 Lebanese and Palestinians and wounded some 30,000 through its military aid to Israel and the Israeli attack in 1982. "But it is not possible to bring back those dead people to life. What should we do now? What are your demands at the present?" the American Muslim delegation asked the hostage holders' representative.

"If those 20,000 were killed by American airplanes and bombs, at least the United States should order Israel not to attack southern Lebanon anymore. Israel attacks Lebanon every other day or week, using American helicopters and American weapons. At least this should be stopped," he pleaded.

"Also, southern Lebanon is occupied by Israel and the United States should ask Israel to pull out of the fifty by six miles of Lebanese territory", he said.

The third demand was that the 800 to 900 Arab Palestinians and Lebanese hostages in Israeli jails should be released before the five to ten American hostages should regain their freedom. "The American news media has not told the American people about the Arab hostages in Israel. These hostages are Palestinians who wish to return to their villages in Palestine. The homes of the Palestinians are occupied by the Jews of Poland or Brooklyn, New York. The Israelis have captured the Palestinians, accused them of infiltration and terrorism and, after a kangaroo style court, imprisoned them for five or ten years and no one will hear about them thereafter," he explained. "To us, these Arab prisoners are all hostages held by the Israelis who are being paid American money, some $15 million a day. "Again," he explained, "these Arab hostages in Israel are being held with American aid and support. These hostages should be released. Then the U.S. should request Kuwait to release the 17 fellow Muslim prisoners in that country."

That first meeting ended without much success, except for the establishment of a measure of dialogue and some give and take by the Muslim Arab delegation and the hostage holders' spokesman. They agreed to meet again and continue the dialogue. The next day the hostage holder did not contact the delegation. This was December 7th. Three days later, contact was established and the first issue raised by the hostage holder was on the question of terrorism. "You call us terrorists, yet your U.S. government in the Security Council of the United Nations refused to condemn Israeli terrorists who had killed four Palestinian students at Beir Zait University."

The U.S. had failed to join the civilized world (Britain, France, U.S.S.R., China and the rest of the members of the Security Council) who had voted to condemn Israel for its killing of the students. It had abstained and, thereby, supported Israeli acts of violence against civilians in Palestine.

As a result, the efforts of the delegation in Beirut were damaged by the U.S. voting in the Security Council of the United Nations in New York. There was a third, brief contact, arranging for further meetings in February 1987.

In February, the delegation, in accordance with the previous arrangements, returned to Lebanon to secure the release of the hostages and to continue the dialogue. However, Lebanon at that period was in the midst of a civil war between "Amal" and "Druze" who had divided West Beirut and engaged in street fighting. Members of the delegation were caught in a crossfire one night and had to hide behind a car for 30 minutes, which seemed to them to be 30 days.

The two fighting factions were exchanging rockets, grenades and machine guns from every which direction against every other direction. Fortunately, members of the delegation were able to escape and spend the rest of the night in the basement of a nearby building.

However, even the Commodore Hotel did not escape the attack of the various fighting factions. It was assaulted by one group and then by the other group. The doors of the hotel were broken, windows shattered to pieces. The fighters attacked the restaurant and stole the television sets, the furniture, plates, silverware and whatever they were able to carry with them.

These attackers were thugs and thieves. They were not motivated by any ideological factor, nor did they have any reaction against the American-Israeli attack on Lebanon in 1982. Their concern was simply to steal as much as they could in order to secure some food for themselves and their families. Most of these fighters were unemployed kids who had not been able to go to school or find any employment and when the various militias of Amal or the Socialist Progressive Party of Druze had asked for volunteers, the young unemployed had joined this or that, received some money and a gun, and then he felt as if he were the law, a government unto himself.

And where do they find their unlimited quantities of ammunition, which they use for no reason whatsoever, except to assert their presence and their strength? A young Lebanese in the uniform of the Progressive Socialist Party of Walid Jumblat (Druze) explained to the delegation that securing ammunition was no problem. The various Arab governments offered the various parties unlimited supplies. And where did those Arab governments get their ammunition? Well, from the arms merchants of the world! On the morrow of the destruction of the Commodore Hotel, members of the delegation walked in the streets of West Beirut, which were full of shells, all kinds of shells, half of which were Russian-made and the other half made in the United States of America!

It was impossible for the members of the delegation to reach the hostage holders. It was, indeed, dangerous to walk in the streets of West Beirut, as shooting and snipers were proceeding continuously from every corner, roof tops or the broken windows of the various shops which had provided some security for the shooters. Moreover, the members of the delegation were robbed in the middle of the night in their hotel rooms of $1400. The robbers were members of the militia, the first group claiming to be from the Druze and the second from Amal and, heaven knows, they were idealogically related to neither. The delegation, being unable to contact the hostage holders, decided to return to the United States.

Of course, the basic difference between the hostage holders and these fighters and thugs was that the first group was ideologically motivated and took its action in reaction to American-Israeli attacks on Lebanon, whereas the warriors in West Beirut were fighting each other, just as various youth gangs in various big cities fight against each other for territorial control of one corner of the town or the other square in the city.

* * *

President Reagan had issued an executive order against travel to Lebanon. But the Arab Muslim delegation had plans to visit with the hostage holders in Beirut, arranged in December 1986. Furthermore, the delegation was traveling to Lebanon on a humanitarian mission, in conformity with the general policy of the United States to secure the release of the hostages. Since the delegation was to engage in a free exchange of ideas and was holding press conferences, the executive order was abridging their First Amendment rights. "The President cannot abridge our freedom of speech and press simply by issuing an executive order," the author told the press. The President should amend the Constitution before he can abridge our First Amendment rights," he said. "This is not a government by decrees, as in Latin America," he protested. "Russia denies its citizens the right to travel abroad and we cannot permit such policies by our own U.S. government," added delegation member Dale Shaheen.

Nevertheless, the United States government confiscated the passport of the author upon his return. Later a new passport was issued to him, but it was stamped "Not valid for travel to Libya or Lebanon." The end result, as of the end of 1987, is that, while the author is possibly the only person who has met with the hostage holders and who speaks their language and understands their thinking, he is denied by the U.S. government to go to Lebanon to secure the release of the American and other hostages.

The U.S. declared policy is to oppose terrorism and secure the freedom of the hostages. To this end, the Reagan Administration designed the policy of arms-for-hostages. Accordingly, arms were sent to Iran to secure the freedom of the hostages in Lebanon. This policy was based on a number of wrong assumptions. The first wrong assumption was the belief that Ayatolah Khomeini of Iran has political authority over the hostage holders in Lebanon. Starting from this basic wrong assumption, other wrong policy actions followed.

Israel had proposed and U.S. policy-makers had accepted the proposal of giving arms to Iran. But Iran was a "terrorist" state and the U.S. was opposed to such states. Hence, a new and strange vocabulary was developed. The concept of "moderate" Iranians was advanced and these "moderate" Iranians were supposedly the recipients of American arms to secure the release of the hostages.

Indeed, in May 1986, a delegation of Americans and their Israeli "guide" had flown secretly to Tehran to negotiate with the so-called Iranian "moderates." The whole irrational policy was as bad as if the Soviets had decided in their policy toward the United States to meet and negotiate with "moderate" Americans, such as Walter Mondale or Guss Hall, rather than with the established government of the United States and President Ronald Reagan!

The policy of the superpower was based on the advice of a few Israeli agents and several unscrupulous arms dealers who, in the interest of Israel and profiteering, had guided the United States to insane policies. That Mr. Reagan and his administration accepted the obscene policy suggestion of arms for hostages is, in part, due to Reagan's obsession with the hostage question. During the 1980 election, he had taunted Jimmy Carter mercilessly concerning the American hostages in the U.S. embassy in Tehran. That bitter attack on Carter has come to haunt him in the form of an obsession concerning the release of the hostages. He was, therefore, ready to accept any advice, absurd or even stupid, if it might in any way help release the hostages in Beirut. To go to the Ayatollah, despite the misgivings, did not sound unreasonable!

However, the hostage holders in Lebanon are under no authority of Khomeini. They may have some spiritual ties to the Ayatollah, but that is similar to the spiritual ties of the American Catholics to the Holy Father in Rome. The spiritual ties of the Roman Catholics will not give any political power to the Pope to dictate certain policies for the Catholics in America. In Lebanon the hostage holders acted on the basis of a Lebanese agenda, not on orders from Khomeini.

Indeed, the hostage holders are a group of individuals exceedingly independent, exceedingly stubborn and they are under the authority of no one, not Khomeini, not Assad and not even their own local religious leader, Mohammad Hussein Fadhlallah. The U.S. policymakers, following the Israeli evaluation and advice, did not consider the Lebanese hostage holders and their agenda and reasons for their action. Naturally, Israel was concerned with its own interests and Israel's interests are not America's interests. Yet the assumption in Mr. Reagan's Washington was that whatever Israel said was correct and a correct evaluation of the Middle East scene. It has been in the interests of Israel to involve America in the Middle East. The Camp David "peace" process brought the U.S. more into the Middle East than ever before. The arms to Iran for hostages in Lebanon was to get the U.S. more deeply involved in the Middle East. Israel succeeded in its designs. When the news of arms for hostages broke out in November 1986, it proved an embarrassment to President Reagan, who had talked again and again about no dealings with the terrorists. Furthermore, the arms to Iran, which was one of the State Department's so-called terrorist states, alienated some of the so-called "moderate" Arab states, who became unhappy that the U.S. had sided with Iran in its war against Iraq. The U.S. now had to change and ingratiate itself to the "moderate" Arabs.

On May 27, 1987, an Iraqi missile hit the USS Stark, killing 37 American sailors. Iraq claimed that it was a mistake and the U.S. simply accepted that explanation. As the result of the Iraqi attack, the White House and the U.S. orchestrated news media started attacking Iran as part of the process to bring the U.S. in closer ties to the Arabs. Then there was the Kiwaiti appeal for symbolic American, Soviet and Chinese ships to protect its oil tankers. The hope was that the three major powers might bring some pressure on Iran and Iraq to stop their ugly war against each other and their crime against humanity, which had resulted in the killing of more than one million of their citizenry.

Mr. Reagan immediately saw "red" in the Kuwaiti plan and felt that that was the beginning of the Communists taking over the Middle East. He offered to the Kuwaiti government a plan of protecting all Kuwaiti oil tankers alone so that the Soviets would be excluded. The end result was that by the end of November 1987 there were more than 100 warships in the Gulf, including mine sweepers, frigates, helicopter carriers, etc. Everyone is tense. Everyone has his fingers on the triggers. And the likelihood of an unintentional attack to create a major war crisis is very much in the working.

The U.S. has been acting as a policeman and, in reality, no one likes a policeman, particularly when he acts as a bully. Such a bully policeman creates resentment among the people of the Middle East, if not the governments of the area. But, to repeat, governments come and go and the people stay. It is much too high a price for America to pay in order to appeal to a few governments and lose the sympathy and respect of the people of those lands.

The President explained that he was sending the American ships to protect the Kuwait oil tankers in order to secure the free flow of oil in the Gulf and in order to prevent the Soviets from dominating the Middle East. But oil was, indeed, flowing freely in the Gulf despite the seven years of the Iraq-Iran war and despite the occasional attack by the various parties on various tankers.

The governments of the Gulf had a gentlemen's agreement not to interrupt the free flow of oil, as oil's free flow meant their own bread and butter. And nobody was ready to stop that flow. However, today there is a greater danger to the free flow of oil in the Gulf than prior to the American involvement.

The President had also stated that if the U.S. does not send its boats, the Soviets will take over. This assumes that the people of the area do not exist or that they are ready and willing to be taken over by the Soviets. If the Soviets try to take over Iran, the Iranians will fight against the Soviet Union and will direct their angers at the Soviets. The Soviets will have their fingers burned, as they are experiencing it in Afghanistan. The Soviets will have another seven years of war in Iran, just as America had its more than seven years of war in Viet Nam. Let the Soviets attack and let them have their Afghanistan in Iran. The U.S. should not deny the Soviets that opportunity!

The problem is that Mr. Reagan does not recognize the power of nationalism in the Middle East and considers the area as a vacuum to be filled either by America or by the Soviets. However, to the people of the area, by far more important than the Americans and the Soviets are themselves. They fight against American interference just as they will fight against the Soviets if the Soviets deny them their nationalism and their right to their sovereignty.

At any rate, if the U.S. is really interested in the free flow of oil, it should call for the reflagging of the oil tankers by the United Nations flag and de-escalate its role in the Gulf. Smaller countries can take their responsibility and if their ships are U.N. reflagged, the likelihood of their being attacked is less than if the ships are U.S. reflagged.

The U.S. reflagging of the ships and taking over the security of the Gulf cannot combat "terrorism," if that is one of the purposes of the United States' international policies. Indeed, such a bullying around of people may increase violence as a reaction to the bully, which, of course, would be decried in western terminology as terrorism.

Let the U.N. supervise the operations in the Gulf. Furthermore, the U.S. should initiate an international arms embargo on the whole of the Middle East so that there would be no American, Soviet, French, British, Italian, North Korean or Chinese arms to Iran or Iraq, Saudi Arabia or other Arab countries or to Israel. Once an international arms embargo is imposed on the whole area, the Iraq-Iran war will have to come to an end and the Israeli occupation of the Golan Heights of Syria, Southern Lebanon, the Taba of Egypt and Palestine will come to an end in the interest of peace in Palestine between all the Jews who wish to stay there and all the Palestinians who wish to return. That will bring the end to the problem of terrorism in Lebanon or at the airports in Rome or elsewhere and throughout the world.

When at Frankfurt Airport, West Germany, authorities arrested a Lebanese who was smuggling a few bottles of explosives and investigation revealed that he was involved in the highjacking of TWA airliner 847, the U.S. government demanded from West Germany to extradite that person, Mohammad Ali Hamadie. Hamadie was from a Lebanese village shelled by the mighty USS New Jersey and the village and its inhabitants were killed and wiped out. Hamadie embarked on a life of retaliation.

The methods of retaliation open to the weak include kidnapping and hijacking, whereas the powerful use jet-fighters, bombs and rockets. TWA flight 847 was the victim and in that airliner Hamadie came across a passenger whom he discovered was a U.S. naval diver.

And immediately Hamadie remembered his village, which was destroyed by the U.S. Navy, USS New Jersey. In fury and emotionalism over remembering the destruction of his family, he loses his head and the poor, innocent Bobby Seate, becomes the victim of Hamadie, who had been the victim of USS New Jersey.

So Hamadie killed Seate in retaliation for what the USS New Jersey had done to his family. Now the U.S. is trying to extradite him for trial and punishment for his killing Seate and hijacking the TWA airliner. The author had appealed to the Department of Justice not to push for the extradition of Hamadie and let him remain a West German problem. The primitive principle of "an eye for an eye" evokes further retributions and further retaliations and is no proper road to solving a problem. War has never been the road to peace.

The cycle of "an eye for an eye" must be broken and someone has to start anew. The strong usually can afford forgetting and forgiving and giving up, while the weak insists on retaliating, on recovering what he considers his right. In the present conflict, the U.S. is the big power and it is in a position to forget. To this effect, the author had advised the Department of Justice here and Chancellor Kohl of West Germany to give Hamadie a speedy trial and to expel him speedily so that further retaliations and further kidnapping by Hamadie's family will not take place.

However, before West Germany was able to give Hamadie a trial and expel him, two West Germans were kidnapped in West Beirut. And West Germany decided not to extradite Hamadie to the United States, to the embarrassment of Attorney General Ed Meese. However, if Meese from the beginning had been more charitable, broad minded, with an international outlook toward the future and had called upon West Germany to try the man, he might not have been embarrased later.

At any rate, the road to combat terrorism is not through punishment and further acts of retaliation which will invoke a greater retribution by the weaker parties against the big power. The road to eliminating "terrorism" is through meeting the human needs of the so-called terrorists to see why they are engaged in their acts and meet their legitimate human demands.

Appendix

Introduction

The following exchange on the air between the author and Rabbi Meir Kahane shows the nature of the conflict and the cause of terrorism. The two parties supposedly speak about the question of Palestine. In reality, they argue about different things. Kahane again and again mentions the Arabs had killed so many Jews in 1927 and before. Or that the Arabs in Iraq and Egypt had done thus and so to the Jews. Also mentioned is the assertion that the Arabs had engaged in slavery and that the Arabs are autocratic, dictatorial and they kill each other.

Assuming that these assertions are correct, would that mean that the Jews of Brooklyn, New York or Los Angeles, California, or Warsaw, Poland have the right to go and occupy Palestine? The attacks on the Arabs here and there will not justify Jewish occupation of Palestine.

The reader will see through this exchange how the Zionists shift the argument from one irrelevant to another irrelevant point. Again and again they attack the Arab character and Arab history as if that would legitimize the Jewish occupation of Palestine.

Of course, in this exchange, as in many, many other such radio and television appearances, invariably the moderator supports the Zionist position and attacks the Arabs. He does so either out of ignorance or out of deliberate prejudice or in order to ingratiate himself to his advertisers.

The following exchange took place on November 3, 1987 in New York over WABC:

BOB GRANT: And, ladies and gentlemen, it was many years ago that we had the first meeting between Meir Kahane and Dr. M.T. Mehdi. Has anything changed since that night in 1978, gentlemen? You were chatting amiably. You're—I'm beginning to worry. You look amiable towards each other.

DR. M.T. MEHDI: Bob, we just decided our different positions. Last night we were both on television and I was introduced as the most moderate Arab and the Rabbi as the extremist. We just decided that he's the most frank Jew and I am the most frank Arab.

GRANT: Well, I don't want to get hung up on labels and I don't want either one of you to feel that you have to live up to a label on this program. I want you to be as honest as you can and, presumably, that means totally frank, totally open. In his book, which I hold in my hand, Rabbi Meir Kahane, in his *Uncomfortable Questions For Comfortable Jews,* talks about the Arab problem in Israel. And Rabbi Kahane, what about that Arab problem in Israel?

RABBI MEIR KAHANE: It's growing. Literally, growing. It's growing in quantity and it's growing in quality. The fact of the matter is that Dr. Mehdi and I both agree that Zionism is incompatible with the rights of Arabs to take away our state from us, either with bullets or with the babies. So Dr. Mehdi believes that Israel, as such, as a Jewish state, really has no right to exist. He's not talking about the West Bank or the First National City Bank. He is talking about Israel as a Jewish state, so he will come and speak about, "Let us all live together, equally and democratically, just like in Syria and, of course, and in Jordan and in Iraq and all those other Arab bastions of democracy. In any case, nothing has changed over all these years. We have agreed to be friendly enemies.

(NOTE: Rabbi Kahane states that, "Zionism is not compatible with the rights of Arabs, et cetera." He means that Zionism is not compatible with democracy. The right of the Arabs to peacefully become a majority is an essential part of democracy and Kahane knows that. And so, instead of stating that Zionism isn't compatible with democracy, he states that it is incompatible with the right of the Arabs to take away the state from the Jews.)

GRANT: I recall, Dr. Mehdi, when you were with Meir Kahane on "The Bob Grant Show" in 1978, I said, "Well, what is it that you want?" And you said you wanted the—and I'll never forget your words—quite, "peaceful withering away of the state of Israel." Do you remember saying that?

MEHDI: I remember saying that, and I have the happy news to relate to you, more and more people across America are accepting our position and this peaceful withering away of the Jewish state will bring peace there for the Arabs, for the Jews and for the international community. More and more Americans are accepting our position, happy to report.

GRANT: Interesting that you talk about America and Americans because there are those who say that the real, the ultimate struggle for the future of Israel is not really in the Middle East but is here in America. What do you think about that statement, Meir Kahane? Does it bother you, as a Jew?

KAHANE: Well, first of all, I don't think that it's true. I think that when Shimon Peres and his parasites, for example, want to have an international peace conference, now... in which we will invite in such objective forces as the Soviets and the Chinese and so on, it's none of their business. And in the end, and I must say this, it's no one's business. Israel will survive or not survive. Israel will solve its problems or not solve them with dialogue between Jews and Arabs. They are the only ones that count. Now I've said many, many times, and I know that Dr. Mehdi will jump in and say, "But America gives Israel three point five billion dollars a year."

First of all, let me make quite clear. On the day that I am the prime minister I am going to ask America to phase out all economic aid to Israel. It doesn't help us. Israel needs private enterprise, free enterprise, capitalism, learn to stand on its own feet and not be a beggar with its hand out to the U.S.A. and the Germans and President Reagan and reparations and all this nonsense.

We have to learn to work hard. We have to learn to build an economy which isn't based upon hand-outs, which adds to the political leverage on Israel. So that is going to stop and Jews will have to learn to work hard again, like it or not, but they will.

GRANT: Dr. Mehdi, you wanted to respond to Meir Kahane. Go right ahead.

MEHDI: Yes, first, I agree with him that the U.S. has been giving Israel—and Israel is America's greatest charity—about fifteen million dollars a day. Stop it. I suggest that America should stop also its military aid to the Arabs. It gives to the Arabs about five million dollars a day in military aid. Unconscionable. Stop it! Don't give it to the Arabs! Don't give it to Israel! Spend it in New York for one day and you will eliminate the tragedy of homelessness. So I agree with the Rabbi that U.S. should stop its military aid to both parties. He didn't say to both parties. I'm adding to both parties. That would be an important beginning for peace in the area.

KAHANE: That is not what I said though.

MEHDI: Yeah. I'm adding—

KAHANE: Economic aid, I said.

MEHDI: Yeah, I know. You are still a militarist. I'm against military aid to both parties.

KAHANE: Wait, wait, wait, wait, wait. The U.S. doesn't give Israel arms or money for weapons because it is charity. The U.S. gives it to Israel because it wants a strong anit-Soviet ally in that region. Now it has a big, big, big choice, of course. Either Israel or Abu Dabi. The point is that Israel gives as much as it gets. The Haifa Naval Base is freely used by the Americans. The Negav is a storage grounds, at this moment, for huge amounts of weapons, U.S. weapons. Israel is an ally of this country. Now I know that you back Jesse Jackson and, therefore, you are backing someone who is an enemy of America. But we who don't like Jesse Jackson, or the Arabs who back Jackson, we are allies of this country.

(NOTE: Kahane claims that Jesse Jackson is an enemy of America. This is really unfair. Jackson has different viewpoints, but if in America we call anyone who has a different viewpoint an enemy of America and proclaim him as a traitor, then the First Amendment is either to be abrogated or becomes completely meaningless. As a matter of fact, the Zionists use such assertions, accusing people of being traitors or anti-Semite in order to throw a "chill" on the right of people to freely express themselves.)

MEHDI: Rabbi, you are not very honest on this because you are really, in the first place, you are—

KAHANE: Dr. Mehdi, that hurt me.

MEHDI: Wait, wait. I'll give you more time to—you are really, and you should be, the ally of Israel. To the extent that you can *use* the U.S., you are doing that, but, in the first place, you should be an ally of Israel and you are. You are using U.S. and now you are also being used by the U.S. as an American base over there.

Now this will create antagonism against America in the Arab world, and I suggest that, in the long run, what America loses is more than whatever it supposedly might gain. Israel is no match to the Soviet Union. If the Soviets wanted to destroy Israel in two minutes, they will do it. So to help Israel and alienate the Arab world, the Muslim world, one billion Muslims is too high of a price to pay because of the politicians here, want to get the Jewish vote.

The politicians are not interested in Israel, nor are they against the Arabs. They're just unscrupulous, trying to get the Jewish vote. Jesse Jackson has the courage, has the frankness and he knows that the future of America is in the Middle East, in the Muslim world, in Asia, in Africa, in Latin America, not in Western Europe nor in Israel.

KAHANE: Jesse Jackson is a demagogue, a fraud, a liar, a racist, an anti-Semite, anti-white. If Jesse Jackson would be white and said just one percent of some of the racist statements that he has made, the B'nai B'rith would be breathing fire. My God, every liberal would be—can you imagine? He would be off the ballot. The Democratic Party would be—would be stoning him. The fact is that there is a double standard in this country. If you're black you can get away with things that no white man could ever say.

MEHDI: Rabbi, that may, in part, be true, but if we—

KAHANE: In part?

MEHDI: —If we collect all the racist remarks that you have made—

KAHANE: I? Dr. Mehdi—

MEHDI: Against the Arabs, against the—

KAHANE: You've pained me again.

MEHDI: —blacks, against the—

KAHANE: Against the blacks? Ohhh. . .

MEHDI: —whites, against the Christians. If we collect all the racist remarks that you have made, you should be excommunicated from the human race!

KAHANE: Doctor, doctor, doctor Mehdi—

MEHDI: Don't interrupt me when I—

KAHANE: Let us not gather all of my statements. Give me one statement that I have made which is anti-black or anti-Christian. One.

MEHDI: Well, let me—

KAHANE: One.

MEHDI: I will give you—last night you talked against the Arabs. The Arabs are—

KAHANE: I never said—against the Arabs.

MEHDI: Okay. And the Arabs are dogs and all—

KAHANE: Dr. Mehdi, I didn't say that they are dogs.

MEHDI: What did you then say? You are becoming as bad as the good Zionists!

KAHANE: Dr. Mehdi, I asked you a question. Answer the question honestly. Name me one statement that was anti-black or anti-Christian.

MEHDI: Your remarks against Reverend Jackson are racist in their essence.

KAHANE: Did I—?

MEHDI: It is an expression of pure hatred.

KAHANE: I don't—I don't—

MEHDI: Well, you asked me a question, so let me answer you.

KAHANE: —attack Jackson because he's black. If Jackson were a blonde Swede I'd say the same thing.

MEHDI: You asked me a question. Let me answer you.

KAHANE: Well, answer it.

MEHDI: Well, don't answer on my behalf. Let me answer it. And then you erudite later if you wish.

GRANT: Erudite? You mean elaborate.

MEHDI: Yeah, I mean, the Rabbi has an ability, a facility with words.

GRANT: Let me ask you a question, Dr. Mehdi. When you came out with that endorsement for Jesse Jerkson (sic), you said you were speaking for eight million Muslims. That's an overstatement. There aren't eight million Muslims in the United States, are there?

MEHDI: Bob, I have the happy news to relate to you that Islam is the second largest religion in America today.

GRANT: Second Largest?

MEHDI: Yes, indeed.

GRANT: Oh, you mean second to Christianity?

MEHDI: Second to Christianity.

GRANT: Alright.

MEHDI: With eight million Muslims, followed by Judiasm, with six million.

GRANT: You don't really regard the so-called black Muslims as real, legitimate Muslims, do you?

MEHDI: No. Under Islam, there are no black Muslims. They're all Muslims.

GRANT. I mean, Farakhan isn't really a Muslim. What does he know? Has he really embraced the Quran? Does he know the Quran? He probably knows as much about the Quran as Jesse Jerkson (sic) does about the New Testament, which isn't much.

MEHDI: Bob, under Islam—

GRANT: If you asked Jesse Jerkson to quote his favorite passage in the Bible, he'd go, "B-b-a-a-a-, well, a-a-h-b-b-b-a, I'll think of it, I'll think of it. Oh yes, here it is. We're gonna go from the out house to the White house."

MEHDI: That is a good imitation of Jackson, but exaggeration too. You are asking a serious question—

GRANT: I'm asking you when you endorsed him, you didn't really mean it. I mean, you're too intelligent a man. You didn't get that doctorate for nothing. You know that he is what Meir Kahane says he is. He is an enemy of his country.

MEHDI: Bob, that is really not fair. In all objectivity, he thinks a little bit differently. And his thinking is with the poor, with the deprived, with the—

GRANT: You really think he cares about the Arabs?

MEHDI: —underdog and with the Third World.

GRANT: Do you really think he cares about it? Do you think he cares about you? You're white.

MEHDI: I think he cares about human beings in the deprived—

GRANT: Your physical appearance is really not much different from Meir Kahane's or mine.

MEHDI: Yeah, of course not.

GRANT: I mean, you are a Caucasian. Therefore, he doesn't like you. He'll use you, but he doesn't like you.

MEHDI: Bob, I am not a Caucasian. I am not a black. I am simply a human being. And that is the case with you and that is even the case with the Rabbi, even if he doesn't like the expression.

KAHANE: But Jesse—you're right. Perhaps that is correct, but Jesse Jackson does not think so. I—I'll go further. Jesse Jackson doesn't really give a damn about poor blacks. I'll go that far. He's a sharp demogogue. This guy, who walks down with thousand dollar suits, he cares about the poor? What're you talking about? He's a demagogue and, worst of all, he will take the position of the Third World against America on every single issue.

MEHDI: Not against America.

KAHANE: Against America.

MEHDI: Because he feels, as I do, that the future of America is more linked with the Third World than with Western Europe, which is the past. It is a new thinking, worth examining, not accusing the man as being anti-American.

GRANT: Yeah, that new thinking, like the new order, like we heard about the new order in the late 1920's and early 1930's. "A new order is sweeping Europe," a man said.

MEHDI: Very bad analogy, Bob—

GRANT: And now you talk about the new—no, not bad analogy.

MEHDI: Very bad analogy, Bob. You know it!

(COMMERCIAL)

GRANT: And we'll go public with Meir Kahane and M.T. Mehdi. It was almost, almost forty years ago—as a matter of fact, if you want to be a stickler for dates, it was November 29, 1947, that the U.N. voted partition, partitioning what was then called Palestine, half Jewish, half Arab. The Arabs began shooting and the Jews, under-

92

standably, shot back. And there hasn't been real peace in the Middle East, in spite of Mr. Sadat's going to Jerusalem and so forth, hasn't been real peace there. Do you think we'll see peace in your lifetime, Dr. Mehdi?

(NOTE: Here, the moderator takes issue and sides with Kahane. He misrepresents the fact that the Arabs started shooting and the Jews, understandably, shot back. After all, it was the Jews who had gone to Palestine and the Palestinians had not gone to the Jewish ghettos of Poland or to the Jewish quarters in New York. The ones who started shooting and committing the first aggression were those who had taken the Palestinians' land and planned to take it over.)

MEHDI: I sure hope so. But peace will depend on the recognition of two important things. The human need of the Jews for a Palestine, for an Israel. And the human rights of the Palestinians to their land. This land should be for all the Jews, including the six million American Jews, if they want to go, let them go. I have no reservation. I want the American Jews to get out of here and go there. Also, the Soviet Jews, the three million of them, let them go there. I have no reservation. But also for all the four million Palestinians.

They will have to stick it out together over there in whatever democratic arrangements, whoever has the majority, to rule the place. That will be recognizing the human need of the Jews for an Israel, the human rights of the Palestinians to their land. And then they will have to fight it out peacefully to have a new go at it. Arms to both parties should be stopped.

GRANT: Fight it out peacefully?

MEHDI: Well, at least they will have to fight it out through voting, through discussions, not warring. And to that extent, that's why I have suggested that the U.S. should stop all its military aid to the Arabs, all its military aid to Israel and there should be an international arms embargo on all of the Middle East so that there'd be no Russian nor Korean, British, French arms to the whole area. That may lead to peace and the recognition of the human conditions of the Jews and the Palestinians, who are entangled in that struggle in the Holy Land.

KAHANE: I will now translate. I will now translate what was said. Obviously, Dr. Mehdi knows that when he, on the one hand, says that Israel has no right to exist as a Jewish state. And then he says that there should be an Israel. However, everybody should be able to live there. He knows that, by weight of sheer numbers, it will not be a Jewish state.

Now Dr. Mehdi, we had eight hundred thousand Sephardic Jews, Jews from Arab countries, who had the tremendous pleasure of living with Arabs together, equally and peacefully, from Morocco to Iraq. And as soon as the state of Israel came into being, they, for some incredible reason, hastily left these bastions of peace. Now, wait a minute Dr. Mehdi, let me just finish. You want to do away with a Jewish state. That will never, never be.

Secondly, when you speak about the Americans and the Russians should stop all shipments of weapons, you know that the Americans might listen to you, but the Russians never, never will. So it's a clever move to have one of the parties stop getting weapons from America and the other party, the Syrians, getting their mig-29's and then their B-30's and 31-hike and that will be that.

Dr. Mehdi, it will not help you. There is a Jewish state just as there are 22 Arab states, God bless them all. We have one state. That will—it will be there forever and ever and you are invited, as Rabbi Meir Kahane's guest as prime minister, to visit Israel any time that you want to.

(NOTE: Kahane states there is one Jewish state and twenty-two Arab states. He fails to say that his one Jewish state was established on the distruction of an Arab state, or Palestine, similar to a statement by a thief who steals some of your property and defends himself by saying that you have more properties. Even worse because the land of the Palestinians belongs to the Palestinians, not to the Arabs of Morocco or the Arabs of Iraq. To take the land of the Palestinians on the ground that other Arabs have other states violates our sense of logic and the human rights of the Palestinians.)

MEHDI: Okay, at present, of course, the Israeli government does not let me go there.

KAHANE: Oh, I will change it. That's outrageous.

MEHDI: Well, okay—

KAHANE: I mean, because they're basically—

MEHDI: Racists. They don't let me. They don't let the Palestinians return.

KAHANE: No, it isn't that. It isn't a racist question, Dr. Mehdi.

MEHDI: Well, whatever. They don't let me in now. The point that you raised, the fear of a Jewish state and the numbers, I say fifteen million Jews to go there. What are you afraid of? Only four million

Palestinians to return to their land? In terms of the number, the Jews will be more and you will have no fear of the Jews becoming a minority.

Now I am suggesting that the twelve, fifteen million Jews of the world to go there. The four million Palestinians to go there. This will assure Jewish majority and if then later there are a few million American Jews who want to go there, to go there. Let the Rabbi think in new terms, not repeating the old cliches and the old formulas which have led us to nowhere. We have to be courageous to think in new terms.

GRANT: Alright—

MEHDI: Hopefully, these will lead to—

GRANT: —let's be courageous and go to the telephones. A lot of people waiting. Isaac, you're on WABC.

ISAAC: Hello, Bob.

GRANT: Yes?

ISAAC: Bob, I was born Jewish in Baghdad, Iraq in 1948, when Israel became a state. All of a sudden there's anti-discrimination against the Jews in Iraq. About maybe—about two hundred religious Jews in Iraq were arrested. One of them was my father. For nothing whatsoever. All the Jews that have left Iraq for Israel, the money, their properties, everything was taken away from them. They let them leave with their shirts and trousers on. Now, I saw Palestinians arriving from Palestine then to Iraq. Homes, Jewish homes, that were left empty were confiscated by the government. Were not used to give the Palestinian refugees. The Palestinian refugees were put in fields and tents to live in—now is that fair? And everybody cries for the Palestinian refugees?

MEHDI: No, that's not fair. But the fact that wrong things done—

ISAAC: In fact, that's what's happened, isn't it? They punish Iraqi Jews. One of them, my father, was arrested for nothing whatsoever.

MEHDI: Isaac, you may be correct.

ISAAC: I'm one hundred percent correct.

MEHDI: Okay, so you are correct. Now what I am suggesting is that it was Rabbi Kahane and the rest of the Zionists—Rabbi Kahane wasn't there in the picture—

ISAAC: —Palestinian refugees. Palestinian refugees, let me tell you, Dr. Mehdi, min-fadlek. (Arabic: please). Palestinian refugees—

MEHDI: Tafeddal (Arabic: Please proceed.)

ISAAC: Thank you. The Palestinian refugees were treated very badly by the Arab countries when they left Israel.

MEHDI: Yeah, and you are correct.

ISAAC: With my own eyes—

(NOTE: Isaac said he was born in 1948. In the same year and next year in 1949 when he was 2 years old, he saw "with his own eyes!")

MEHDI: You are correct.

ISAAC: I've seen with my own eyes. So what are you talking now that Israel does not—all those people who left the Middle East, the Arab countries, went to Israel. Israel accepted them with open arms. But the Arab countries would not accept Palestinian refugees with open arms. They put them—they let them live in the street, the tents. They didn't give them food. Meanwhile, they took all the money of the Jews, all their properties, everything, and then the Jews got out with their shirts and trousers. What do you think of that?

NOTE: Isaac compares two different sets of events, which are the result of different factors, and, therefore, have no resemblance to each other except in name. That the Jews left the Arab countries should be evaluated in terms of its own right or wrong. It is no substitute for what Jews do to the Palestinians in Palestine. The Jews of Iraq have their rights to Iraq, just as the Palestinians have their rights to the land of Palestine. The "collectivist" mentality of the Zionists puts apples and oranges together and evaluates one in terms of the other. If, as Isaac says, the government of Iraq had confiscated Jewish homes and had put the Palestinians in tents and farms, that is a problem for which the Iraqi government should be accountable. But the discussion here is about Palestine rather than about the bad behavior of the government of Iraq.

Furthermore, the Jews of Iraq were supposedly going "home," replying to the call of Zionism. However, the Palestinians were being kicked out of their home, which was Palestine.)

MEHDI: Isaac. The difference is that the Israeli leaders had told the Jews who were in Iraq that you are foreigners in Iraq. That you are foreigners in exile in Egypt. "Come home." So it was the Israeli leaders of the Zionist movement who called for that—Today they would—want to uproot the Soviet Jews to go there. They would rather later uproot the American Jews to go there.

KAHANE: But Doctor Mehdi, but Doctor Mehdi, you also said that. You just moments ago said that let there be Israel and let the Jews of Russia come there and American Jews come there. And now you say, "But they're not foreigners. They're Americans. And they're Russians and so on."

MEHDI: That is the Zionist thinking. That is the Zionist philosophy that says American Jews are residing in exile.

KAHANE: But, therefore, that's exactly my point. The kind of state that you call for, you know that the Jews of this country will not go there.

MEHDI: Because they are not stupid.

KAHANE: That's exactly right. And, therefore, I am not stupid either. And, therefore, we will never allow your kind of a state.

(COMMERCIAL)

GRANT: Here we are on WABC and we'll say hello to Raja for Mr. Kahane and for Mr. Mehdi. Yes, Raja.

RAJA: Yes, good afternoon, Mr. Grant. I would like to congratulate Mr. Mehdi for a good job he's done so far and I congratulate him for telling the truth and telling, you know, the right situation about the Middle East.

MEHDI: Thank you very much.

RAJA: Excuse me?

MEHDI: Thank you very much.

RAJA: Oh, thank you, sir. And I would like to ask Mr. Mehdi, why would he support a Democrat? Why not Republicans like Mr. Bush or, you know, Mr. Dole or somebody else?

MEHDI: On the whole, the Democrats, I think, are more with the people at large, with the needs of the American society, with the poor people, on the whole, on the whole, from the Roosevelt era, than the Republicans, who are more with the big business, on the whole. Not necessarily—

RAJA: But aren't the Republicans more supportive of the Muslim world and the Arab world or, you know, the rights of Palestinians than the Democrats?

MEHDI: Not at all. Both of them are almost equally bad because they are ignorant. They really don't know much about the Muslim world. Hardly any of them knows that the Muslin world is composed of more than one billion human beings, which is one-fourth of the human race. And—

KAHANE: One-fifth of the human—

MEHDI: It is five billion, a billion and two hundred million Muslims is about one-fourth of the human race. Jesse Jackson understands this more. He related himself to the people here at large, to the poor people here at large, to the deprived people here at large and on the international scene, to the Third World. That is why we believe that he will be more the link between the America of now and America's future, a few years from now.

RAJA: Thank you, sir, and I salute your courage and wisdom.

GRANT: Where are you from Raja?

RAJA: I was born in the Islamic Republic of Pakistan and I'm a citizen of the United States.

GRANT: Pakistan, eh?

RAJA: Thank you, Mr. Mehdi.

GRANT: I think General Zia's looking for you. He wants to put you right next to—I guess he's hung up. That's the mentality of that part of the world, right? Right. Here we have Mohammad.

MOHAMMAD: Yeah, hi, Bob. I've called you before and I congratulate you for inviting the two guests here. Very important men. And I have a question for Rabbi Kahane.

KAHANE: Yes, sir.

MOHAMMAD: Rabbi, I say that you're an honest person really and I have respect for you for being honest. But then I also want to say this thing. That when you go to the West Bank or to the Arab population of Israel, with people around you with machine guns, threatening them to leave, are you going to push them in the sea? Are you going to kill them, whatever?

Did you ever think even once that that's what Hitler wanted to do with the Jews and that's what Hitler was doing in Germany? And don't you realize this thing, that Hitler, therefore, can be said to be the benefactor of Israel and, unfortunately, the militant and the extremist people like you, that number one, he helped create the guilt complex in the Americans and the Europeans that justifies the support to Israel. And number two, that you are following and you're paying the biggest tribute to Hitler, following in his footsteps. And don't you think it's a good idea to have a monument in downtown Tel Aviv of Hitler so that the passing Jews can leave flower on it?

KAHANE: Is that it?

MOHAMMAD: That's it.

KAHANE: Now you just listen, you creep. Listen here.

MEHDI: Don't be abusive, Rabbi.

KAHANE: Doctor Mehdi—

GRANT: He's not being abusive. He's being descriptive.

KAHANE: Listen here, Doctor Mehdi. Up until now we've sat here quietly. What a disgraceful outrage for you to sit there and hear this animal talk about a monument to Hitler and you sit there quietly. Now you be quiet while I answer him.

MEHDI: Don't be discourteous.

KAHANE: I will be as discourteous to this animal as I want to be. And Doctor Mehdi, now you be quiet now. It is my turn. He spoke to me and not to you.

MEHDI: Yeah, but be nice.

KAHANE: I will be nice to that worm?

MEHDI: Bob, Bob, Bob. Human beings are not worms!

GRANT: Even you should have been offended by that last statement. Monument to Hitler—

MEHDI: That is what Zionism is the product of, Nazism.

GRANT: Go ahead, Meir.

MEHDI: Go ahead.

KAHANE: The point is, you lowlife out there, in the 1920's, long before there was a Kahane or a Jewish state, Arabs were massacring Jews in what you called Palestine. In the 1930's, they were massacring Jews. In one day in 1929 sixty-seven Jews were murdered in cold blood. Hebron. In 1947, when you could have had your Palestine, had you followed the U.N., and the Jews accepted a partition plan. Accepted a tiny little state, you people said, "No." And you people went to war and you killed Jews, you creep out there. And now you talk about Jews, about Jews murdering Arabs. I don't want to murder Arabs. I want every Arab in Israel to live happily and peacefully elsewhere because I know what you will do to us tomorrow because I know what you did to us yesterday.

(NOTE: Kahane is offended that Israel should raise a monument to Hitler. As a matter of fact, the real father of Israel is Hitler even more than Herzel. And Israel is a by-product of anti-Semitism even more than Zionism. Hitler was able to succeed where Herzel had failed. Anti-Semitism was more powerful a force in getting the Jews to Palestine than Zionism ever could have been. So to maintain that Israel owes much of its existence to Hitler and anti-Semitism is simply mentioning a fact, even though the Zionists do not like the fact and even though they capitalize on it and milk it continuously.

But the substantive answer that Kahane provides in his reply to the caller, Mohammad, is of interest. His answer is by attacks on the Arabs in the 1920's and the 1930's and 1947, the usual style of shifting the argument and talking about the old cliches.)

99

(COMMERCIAL)

GRANT: On WABC, let's get back to our phones. And this time we'll say hello to Robert. Hello, Robert.

ROBERT: Yes, Bob. Hello, Bob?

GRANT: Yes, go ahead.

ROBERT: I have two questions. I'd appreciate I could just ask them and then you could both not interrupt and I'll hang up the phone.

GRANT: No, no, no, no. You don't hang up the phone. Just ask your question. Go ahead.

ROBERT: Doctor Mehdi, you propose that the Jews and the Palestinians live in one state together and, you know, try and work out their differences in that scenario. How could you propose that when you are against Zionism? How could you have two people living side by side, living in peace, when you don't even recognize those people that are Zionists or Jews? That can't possibly be.

In other words, how could you have a state where two people are living in the same area and yet they're both opposed to each other and you're for abolishing that state? Number two, I have a question for three of you, representing all different faiths of Christianity, Judaism and Islam. In this Middle East today, there are twenty-one foreigners, nine of them being Americans, being held by Islamic fundamentalists. My question to the three of you is more of a soul searching question. How could the world sit there and support Arab causes and the people, like Dr. Mehdi, that spew peace, when the people that he is representing are torturing Americans, literally killing them? They held about fifty Americans hostage for over a year and a half. And yet this man sits there and talks about how Israel is using the U.S., when Americans are, literally, right now slaving away and dying there.

(NOTE: Caller Robert refers to the hostages. He asks how could the world sit there and support the Arab cause. The Arabs are torturing Americans. Literally, killing them.

Assuming that some Arabs are "torturing Americans, literally, killing them," as Robert suggests, does this mean that other Arab rights should not be supported and should not receive the backing of the people of the world? If some Arabs are doing certain wrong things, they should be condemned. But that does not mean that, therefore, the Jews of Los Angeles have the right to occupy Palestine and commit atrocities in Palestine. The wrong deeds against the Americans in Lebanon, for what-

100

ever reasons, will not justify Jewish occupation of the land of the Pales-
tinians. This Robert does not seem to understand.)

GRANT: Alright, Robert. Thank you very much. It's a good question. Gentlemen.

MEHDI: Robert, thank you for the question. I don't know whether it was good or otherwise. At any rate, how can I propose that the fifteen million Jews live in Palestine with the four million Palestinians? I can because I hope that Zionism will tame, will be modernized, will be humanized and so would Arab nationalism become a little more humane, recognizing the human need of the Jews to be there.

I have hopes for a better tomorrow. And, of course, they will have many difficulties, but their problems, at worst, are not as bad as the permanent war situation of today. As to your second question, we are, of course, all opposed to holding hostages. I, personally, had gone to Lebanon at a great risk, personal risk, to secure the release of the hostages. But when these terrorists hold hostages, they are reacting to greater terrorism of America supporting Israel which killed twenty thousand Lebanese. It is—the whole act should be condemned. The holding of the hostages should be condemned and the Israeli-American's killing of twenty thousand Lebanese and Palestinians to be condemned. And then we'll be fair and can hope for the release of the hostages and some justice for all.

GRANT: Rabbi Kahane?

KAHANE: And now the truth. Listen, Doctor Mehdi. Listen to me.

MEHDI: Rabbi Kahane's way?

KAHANE: The Lebanese war is a civil war, began not in 1982 but in 1976, if not earlier. The Moslems have killed Christians and Christians have killed Moslems, both have killed Druze, Druze have killed both. You sit and you babble about co-existence between Jews and Arabs. Meantime, I'm waiting for co-existence between Arabs and Arabs, Shiites and Sunnis and Druze and Christians, Hezballah. Each one massacres the other one. What are you talking about? America helps Israel kill Arabs in Lebanon? Arabs kill Arabs in Lebanon.

(NOTE: In "refuting," the assertion that the Lebanese have been holding American hostages as a result of the 1982 Israeli attack on Lebanon with American weapons, Kahane states that Arabs have been killing Arabs, Christians against Christians and Muslims against Muslims as far back as 1976.

Here again, Kahane is skirting the question and bringing in different

101

issues. It is true that Arabs have been killing Arabs. But this does not negate the fact that the hostage holders have been taking American hostages, as the result of their reaction to American support of Israel, and the Israel killing of some twenty thousand Lebanese and Palestinians in the 1982 attack on Lebanon. The two things are not mutually exclusive. Arabs had been killing Arabs. And Arabs are holding American hostages because of the Israeli atrocities in Lebanon with the help of the American military might)

MEHDI: That is true. Some Arabs have killed—

KAHANE: Some? Some a hundred and fifty thousand is quite a bit of some.

MEHDI: Okay, Rabbi, that is your figure. At any rate, if Arabs have killed Arabs, is bad, but America helping Israel to kill twenty thousand Arabs is equally bad.

GRANT: Let's take another phone call. Dorothy, hello.

DOROTHY: Hello, Bob? Hello?

GRANT: Alright, we're listening.

DOROTHY: Yes, I had a call on the New York line. I couldn't get through. Mr. Mehdi?

MEHDI: Yes, Dorothy.

DOROTHY: I—

MEHDI: I know your voice. I hear it in Los Angeles and elsewhere.

GRANT: She's got your number.

MEHDI: I've got hers too..

DOROTHY: Mr. Mehdi?

MEHDI: Yes, Dorothy.

DOROTHY: Let me correct—

MEHDI: Mrs. Dean.

DOROTHY: Yes, let me correct several false statements you made. First of all, you said that most Americans now are sympathizing with your viewpoint. Not only is that a lie, but I have the facts to prove it. Just recently, the entire Senate, from Senator Kennedy to Senator Dole to Senator Jesse Helms, insisted that the PLO offices in America must be closed. The one in Washington and the one in New York at the U.N. And only in a compromise did the Administration agree to kick the PLO out of Washington and they're leaving the one in New York alone temporarily.

The entire American Congress knows the PLO for what it is. It's a terrorist organization. So American support is increasing for Israel, not for your viewpoint. That's number one. Number two, at the U.N., every year at the U.N. the Arabs bring up a resolution: throw Israel out. This happens every year. Now this year they did it again. But surprise, eighty-nine to thirty-nine, the Arabs were defeated and the rest of the U.N. abstained.

GRANT: Alright, Dorothy. Thank you. We're going to ask Rabbi Kahane, Doctor Mehdi, to stay with us, so you stay with us on WABC.

(NEWS)

GRANT: If you've just tuned in, we have held over, by popular demand, Rabbi Meier Kahane, controversial member of the Israeli Parliament, Founder of the JDL, and Doctor M.T. Mehdi, President of the American-Arab Relations Committee. He has also named himself the Secretary General of the National Council on Islamic Affairs. He has a meeting with that organization every afternoon in a phone booth. Right now we're going to check in with Bob Williams and WABC Shadow Traffic.

(TRAFFIC REPORT)

GRANT: Alright, let's get back to our telephones here on seventy-seven, WABC. Do you want to withdraw your support of Jesse Jerkson (sic), by the way?

MEHDI: Bob, it is discourteous on your part to make the name of the man sound discourteously. The man's name is Jackson, so say Jackson. That's all. Then say, Jackson that I don't like. But don't abuse the name. Particularly earlier, you made the crack about our National Council on Islamic Affairs, which reaches—we have eight million American Muslims. The members of our organization presently are four thousand Muslim M.D.'s, all over the country. Anyway, a word or two about Dorothy, the eternal Dorothy, who calls. She's correct that the Senators and the politicians in Washington have to cater to the Jewish vote so they would be willing to subvert the First Amendment—

GRANT: She didn't say that. She didn't say they have to cater to the Jewish vote—

MEHDI: No, I am explaining it. So they decided—

GRANT: But you're making it sound as though that's what she said. Now that's unfair.

MEHDI: No—Dorothy—

GRANT: And sneaky. That is sneaky.

MEHDI: If that—if you thought that that is what I said, I am sorry. I did not say that. You said, "Dorothy said that Congressmen and

Senators are against the PLO." True. But that is not the American public opinion. The public opinion, at large, all over the country is changing and gradually is accepting our position. Sooner or later it will reflect—

GRANT: The American public—

MEHDI: —on the whole . . .

GRANT: The American public does not accept the PLO, does not approve of the PLO, is well aware the PLO is a terrorist organization with murder in its soul.

MEHDI: Bob, that was your speech in the past. You will have to change it. Because the people are really changing. Believe me.

GRANT: You mean the PLO is changing?

MEHDI: The American public is more—their common sense makes them appreciate that they were lied to by the media, by the President—

GRANT: Yassir Arafat has changed?

MEHDI: No. Yassir Arafat—

GRANT: In other words, he's still a murdering skunk?

MEHDI: He is trying to liberate his land from the murderers who have occupied his land—

GRANT: His land?

MEHDI: Yes, indeed. Of course. Palestine was not the land of Menachim Begin or Poland or Rabbi Kahane of Brooklyn. These have gone to Palestine, occupied it and the Palestinians do not—

GRANT: You made a little remark, Meir Kohane of Brooklyn.

MEHDI: Of course. Meir Kohane was—

GRANT: Is that like M.T. Mehdi of Baghdad?

MEHDI: No, they are different. Because when I came to the United States, I came with the permission of the American people. Rabbi Kahane, when he went to Palestine, he and his colleagues went over there against the will of the people of Palestine.

GRANT: I don't believe he's ever been in Palestine. I do believe, however, he made allya and went to Israel.

MEHDI: Yeah, his colleagues had occupied that land. I have a little bit of news for you, which the Rabbi doesn't know. Today, November 3rd, 1987, is the 800 Anniversary of the liberation of Jerusalem from the Crusaders. That is in the year 1187, Jerusalem was liberated after it had been occupied by—

KAHANE: You mean by Saladdin?

MEHDI: By Salahuddin. Today is that historic day and—

KAHANE: Eight hundred years—?

MEHDI: —the same Jerusalem will be also liberated—

KAHANE: Eight hundred years?

MEHDI: Ago. Right.

KAHANE: I'm impressed. Now I have news for you, which you may not know. Hanacha is coming. It is the two thousand three hundredth year of the time when the Macabbes, who were Jewish and were living in a country, defeated the Greeks.

MEHDI: Good for them.

KAHANE: Good for Saladdin. Listen to me. Saladdin came into a country which was ours, Jewish. We unfortunately, had been thrown out through no fault of our own. The Romans threw us out. Not a day passed, Dr. Mehdi, when Jews did not pray three times a day as they faced Jerusalem, not Mecca, as Moslems do. Jerusalem, for us to come back. And we came back. We came back and we are there. And we will always be there and you can be there too when I allow you in.

(NOTE: Again, Kahane lives in the past. The assertion that "the Romans threw us out," is so funny. Remembering that the ancestors of the majority of European Jews, including possibly Kahane himself, were Slavs or from among some of the other Eastern European tribes, it is absurd for Kahane to say that the Romans threw them out.

Then the fact that Jews had prayed toward Jerusalem, that does not impose any obligation on the Palestinians to give up their homes. This doesn't seem to make sense to Kahane and the Zionists. Their claim will not impose any obligation on the other party to accept the validity of that claim.)

MEHDI: Rabbi, you will be interested to know that when Salahuddin came eight hundred years ago today to Jerusalem, the few Jews who were there welcomed the arrival of the Muslim—

KAHANE: A big, big choice they had.

MEHDI: —as did the—of course, of course—défeated European Crusaders.

KAHANE: A big, big choice they had.

MEHDI: —as the liberators. You are so ungrateful. What shall I say?

(NOTE: The European Crusaders waged some two hundred years of war on Islam. During their occupation of Syria, Lebanon, and Palestine, they rampaged the land and killed the "infidels" who stood in their way. They succeeded in establishing the "Latin kingdom of Jerusalem," which lasted for some fifty years. On November 2, 1187, Jerusalem was

liberated by Salahuddin and his fellow Muslims. The victorious Muslims treated the vanquished Europeans with respect and honor. Salahuddin considered the European Christians as brothers in monotheism, "people of the Book." He gave them the choice between returning to their European countries of origin if they wished, with facilities provided by the Muslims, or to stay in the Holy Land for religious purposes. The Crusaders' State lasted some fifty years. That was the first manifestation of European colonialism in the name of Jesus.

The recent Zionist invasion in the name of Moses is the second manifestation and the modern state of Israel has lasted for forty years. There are ten more years to go.)

KAHANE: Doctor Mehdi, the poor Jews there, the hapless Jews, Jews there, would have welcomed anyone in the fervent hope that he wouldn't kill them. Nobody welcomed Moslems there because they wanted to.

MEHDI: Rabbi, you really are unfair and ungrateful. The Jewish civilization, the height of it was with the Muslims in Spain and their contribution to humanity—

KAHANE: The yellow badge originated under Moslems in Spain and not under Christians in Europe. Know that. Know that.

MEHDI: Rabbi, you are unfair and historically wrong. The height of Jewish contribution to humanity was with the Muslims because Islam believes in Judaism, in Christianity and a Muslim is not a Muslim if he does not believe in Judaism. A Muslim is not a Muslim if he does not believe in Christianity. So please, let's admit the good—

KAHANE: Doctor Mehdi, please, please, please, please. Under the Moslems, no non-Moslem can be equal to Moslems. That is a fact and I happen to know that you are not one of the great believers. Last night on a show, a TV show, you said anyone who believes that God gave, you know, the Jewish people their land, it's madness, it's insanity. You are not one of the great believers.

MEHDI: No, I said the Jews who believe that God was a real estate man, gave them this land three thousand years ago—

KAHANE: Doctor Mehdi—

MEHDI: —after Joshua had captured Jericho, killed every man, woman and child there and—

GRANT: Do you reject the covenant with Abraham, is that what you reject?

MEHDI: No, I really think the whole thing is such a mythology, has no basis—

GRANT: When you say the whole thing, you mean religion is a mythology.

MEHDI: As interpreted by the Jews claiming that God gave it to them and told them to kill everyone in Jericho. That is—

KAHANE: What about the Quran?

MEHDI: The Quran says Judaism is a religion of God, Christianity is a religion of God. So that's alright. But God is not a real estate man.

KAHANE: Sir, did the angel Gabriel really come and give this book to your prophet? Was he really a prophet? Or was it a mythology? Tell us. Which is the mythology and which isn't?

(NOTE: Kahane is asking whether Angel Gabriel did bring the book to the prophet.

This is another case of diverting the issue from the main subject. The subject of discussion was the right of the Jews to occupy Palestine and establish a Jewish state, rather than whether Gabriel did or did not bring the book to the prophet Mohammad. When the author criticized Joshua 6, verse 21–25, that God had asked Joshua to kill every man, woman and child in Jericho, that was not a criticism of the Bible. It was the criticism of an issue relevant to the question of war and peace in Palestine today. If anyone really believes in the mythology that God had told Joshua to kill the people in Jericho, then that really presents the picture of a tribal God, not the universal God whom people worship.)

MEHDI: The point really is that a real estate guy giving this land to somebody to justify their existence—

KAHANE: Is the Quran also a myth or just the Jewish and Christian Bible? Tell us where the myth starts and where it stops. Tell—

MEHDI: At least here and for the purposes here, the myth that God asked Joshua to kill every man, woman and child in Jericho is a myth, is absurd to blame it on the good Lord. It is the evil that men do and then blame on God. We should be ashamed of ourselves for that use of God.

GRANT: You can blame me for interrupting because it's fourteen minutes now past four o'clock.

(COMMERCIAL)

GRANT: Back to our phones and, of course, Meir Kahane and M.T. Mehdi and Marty. You're on WABC. Hello.

MARTY: Thank you, Bob, for having a counter-voice against that Arab fascist voice which we hear quite often. Rabbi Kahane, I haven't seen you since you had the JDL meeting at Brooklyn College in 1967.

KAHANE: Good God, that's—

MARTY: I remember it.

KAHANE: —a long time ago.

MARTY: Yes. Now I want to talk about that Arab fascist there. He was on a talk show once and I brought up the subject, which might have missed you, about the 600 Jews that were hanged in the square of Baghdad in 1940 for one reason. They were Jewish. And he said, "Yeah, I deplore that. I thought it was bad." Yeah, of course. Now the Quran in Sura 5, clause 61 and Sura two, clause 51 says the Jews and Christians are to be humiliated. If anyone—any Moslem who cohabits with them and is nice to them will not enter Paradise. Jews are to be taxed and humiliated. At all times they are to pay taxes where no one else does and to be beaten while they do it.

(NOTE: Marty is simply lying. Sura five, verse sixty-one reads, "When they (unbelievers) come unto you (Muslims), they say, we believe; but they came in unbelief and they went out in the same; and Allah knows best what they were hiding." And Sura two, verse fifty-one reads, "And when We did appoint for Moses forty nights (of solitude) and then ye chose the calf, when he had gone from ye, and were wrongdoers."

Verse fifty-two: "Then, even after that, we pardoned you in order that you might give thanks."

Verse fifty-three: "And when We gave unto Moses the scripture and the Criterion of right and wrong, that he might be led aright. . ."

Verse fifty-four: "And when Moses said unto his people, 'Oh my people, ye have wronged yourselves by your choosing of the calf (for worship). So turn in pentence to your Creator and kill the guilty (yourselves). That will be best for you with your Creator and He will relent toward you. Lo, He is relenting, the merciful."

There are none of the assertions attributed by Marty to the Quran.)

MARTY: Now I would suggest that that Arab fascist, the creep, read Bernard Lewis, Professor Bernard Lewis, of Princeton, with *The Jews of Islam*. And he'll find a lot of things that—he keeps talking will not happen. He doesn't mention them. That they'll live pleasantly when, in truth, Jews for 800 years were not allowed to walk on the same side of a street as an Arab, had to wear distinctive garb, lead weights around their neck. A pregnant Jewish woman could be stoned to death. And the only way you could get a conviction if someone—a witness brought it up.

(NOTE: Again, Professor Bernard Lewis's book does not contain any

of the assertions of Marty. He is lying again and misrepresenting this author.

However, assuming that all these assertions are correct, does that mean that the Jews of Kiev, USSR have the right to go and occupy Palestine and kill a single Palestinian or occupy a single inch of the Palestinian land?)

MARTY: In fact, they came to the tax collector and they were beaten. They had to hold their hands up and they were beaten. They had to buy foul meat, which was not kosher, which spoiled at the end of the day. And there must be a reason why almost every Jew has left every Arab land. Because they couldn't exist in those places. And this—you want to say we live side by side? It appears to me you are an unmitigated liar and a propagandist. You sound like a Goebbels trained man.

MEHDI: Okay, are you through with your garbage? You really should be ashamed of yourself, misquoting the Quran and misrepresenting it. As to fascism, possibly the whole concept of Zionism, to take over some other people's land and establish a racist state, is closer to fascism than any other doctrine today. But for heaven's sake, do not misrepresent the Quran. Bernard Lewis is more intelligent than the misrepresentations that you have made of his book. Do not be discourteous. You disagree with me. That's fair enough. But don't make yourself obscene in your explanation. As to the Jews who were in the Arab world, I told you. If they were mistreated, they were killed, I am against that mistreatment. What's wrong with that? But the Jews who are now out of their countries, most of them long to return back to Baghdad and Damascus and Cairo.

KAHANE: Doctor Mehdi, I am just stunned here. You're upset because this person made comments about your Bible, your Quran. You sat there five minutes ago and said that large parts of the Torah, or the Jewish Bible, are myths. What an outrage that was. If you give it, fellow, you have to learn to also take it because we Jews have long since stopped just taking it. We also give it.

(NOTE: Again, Kahane misrepresents and shifts the argument. He claims that the author had said that "large parts of the Torah and the Bible" are myths. In reality, and to repeat, the author had simply stated that Joshua six, verse twenty-one, which claims that God had ordered Joshua to commit the first act of genocide in recorded history, that was ugly and shameful. He had said nothing about the Bible, the Old or the New Testaments, large or small parts thereof.)

MEHDI: Rabbi, when I say—people have to examine the validity of this God according to Joshua six, verse 21—God asked Joshua to enter Jericho, kill every man, woman and child, the ox, the donkey and set the city afire. If this God really did so, this is an ugly God. As a—

GRANT: Why do you dwell, why do you dwell on that—?

MEHDI: —matter of fact, God didn't. It is those Jews who blamed it on God.

GRANT: Why do you dwell on one passage of the Bible? There are so many passages. You know, you could have picked Isaac and Abraham, where—

MEHDI: Very good—

GRANT: Didn't God save Isaac? He told Abraham to have trust and Abraham had trust—

KAHANE: Yes, but that's nothing you prove here. Wait—But what do you call the covenant? There is a clear covenant between God and Abraham, giving the land to Abraham. Why do you say that that's a myth?

MEHDI: If given to Abraham, it is to the Arabs even more than Menachim Begin of Poland.

KAHANE: My dear fellow, that's why you don't know the Bible because you are—

MEHDI: I know the Bible possibly as much as you do, if not a bit more. My interpretation is different than yours.

KAHANE: Doctor Mehdi, you know, it's one thing to be ignorant. It's one thing to be arrogant.

MEHDI: It's another thing to be a Rabbi.

KAHANE: But for someone who is an arrogant, ignorant person, don't tell me that you know my Bible better than I do.

MEHDI: Rabbi, let me—

KAHANE: Because that really, really makes you quite a fool. Now you have your field of expertise and I would not presume to state that I know that better. But please, a Rabbi who studied for years and years and years in his field, please, a little bit, you know, be a bit humble. In the same Bible, it states quite clearly that Ishmael would be given great power and twelve princes will come from him, but that the covenant would go through Isaac only.

MEHDI: That is your interpretation of it, but—

KAHANE: Doctor Mehdi, open Genesis, chapter seventeen. It's

not an interpretation. It's black and white. It's written in clear Hebrew or English.

GRANT: Alright—let's say hello to Morty. Morty, welcome to the fray.

MORTY: Yes, gentlemen, good afternoon.

MEHDI: Good afternoon to you, Morty.

MORTY: And I'm not surprised that you were the only one that said good afternoon because I've, you know, spoken to Bob always does, if I may say that. Meir Kahane always throws out a lot of rhetoric and I expect a lot of it now. You call Dr. Mehdi, he's a terrorist—

KAHANE: I didn't say that. You did, fella.

MORTY: Oh. It's not fella. It's Morty. You are a Rabbi. And I will call you that.

KAHANE: Okay, Morty. You said it and I didn't okay? So let's—so, therefore, let's stick to facts and not to rhetoric. Okay?

MORTY: Okay. Now I call Mr. Sharon, a terrorist. Menachim Begin, a terrorist. Moshe Dayan and, you know, so on.

KAHANE: And Arafat, too, right?

MORTY: You've also said that you are—if you are elected that you don't need the United States' six billion dollars—

KAHANE: How much is it now?

MORTY: Six.

KAHANE: It's become pregnant I see.

GRANT: It's not six billion a year.

MORTY: Well, let me finish. As you always say to me, "Shhh or we'll cut you off." Your favorite line. Okay? Now you said that you would swim to the United States if you won because, you know, we don't need the money.

KAHANE: I said what?

MORTY: I have it on tape from another show.

KAHANE: Tell me, tell me again. Again.

MORTY: You know, don't be the kind that answers a question with a question, which is your stock in trade.

KAHANE: That is a—

GRANT: You haven't asked him a question.

MORTY: You are a Rabbi. I am Morty. Bob Grant is Mr. Grant.

GRANT: You are a liar.

MORTY: I'm a liar?

GRANT: That's right.

MORTY: Okay. I have it on tape. But whatever, if you would allow me to finish.

GRANT: Go ahead. Please, please do. Please.

MORTY: The question that I have is that you call other people terrorists.

KAHANE: Who'd I called a terrorist today?

MORTY: Would you let me finish?

KAHANE: No. Who'd I called a terrorist?

MEHDI: Arafat, for example.

KAHANE: And Morty, is Yassir a terrorist or not?

MORTY: I would say so, but you are in the same category. What does JDL do? But let me get to my point. This is your typical thing. Rile somebody up so he forgets what he wanted to say.

KAHANE: Well, calmly, calmly—

MORTY: Let me get to the point.

KAHANE: Be calm. Be calm, fella. Be calm.

MEHDI: Rabbi, please. Rabbi, please. You be calm. Let him talk.

GRANT: He's calm. I'm looking at him. He's calm.

MEHDI: Yeah, but interrupting the man—

MORTY: What I am saying is that there are more than one terrorist in the Middle East, okay? And the so-called junkie that is feeding the Middle East, if you did not have our tax dollars, they would have been up the creek a long time ago, okay? And you talk about Abraham, okay. It was promised to those that follow and come from the seed of Abraham. Okay, Arabs and Jews are brother and sister, if you read your book. But, of course, your interpretation is not as such. Okay, you go around and you say that you're an orthodox Rabbi, which I'm sure you are. And you know the book. But it's twisted to your interpretation. Okay, my question is why can't we call a spade a spade that they are not the only terrorists. Yes, Yassir Arafat is a terrorist. And you call yourself freedom fighters. Let's get the record straight because if the fighting continues to go on, one is gonna destroy the other and who the hell is gonna win? No one.

GRANT: Alright. Wish we had time to address all this, but Meir Kahane, if you'll hold that thought, we'll respond to Morty, who's a very curious fellow, to say the least. At twenty-six minutes past four o'clock.

(COMMERCIAL)

GRANT: Alright, this is the Bob Grant program, although at times if you get confused and wonder, I don't blame you. We are listening to, engaging in a conversation really between Mohammad Mehdi, Dr.

M.T. Mehdi, president of the American-Arab Relations Committee, and Rabbi Meir Kahane. And if there's anybody from National Hillel in this vast Bob Grant audience, would you please have the *chutzpah*, the temerity, to tell me why you have a national letter out to every Hillel chapter on every college campus barring, forbiding, proscribing the scheduling of Meir Kahane. Explain yourselves.

MEHDI: And the ADL, why don't they have the guts to sit with me to discuss these issues? They also have the same kind of thing, the Anti-Defamation League, against me.

GRANT: Lou, you're on WABC. Good afternoon.

LOU: Hello, Bob, you ought to get a piece of AT&T and I wish they'd run those commercials in high speed. What a wait. Dr. Mehdi, I have a few questions for you.

MEHDI: Yes, sir.

LOU: Firstly, are you a citizen of the United States?

MEHDI: Yes, sir.

LOU: You are? Well, I wasn't clear on that.

GRANT: Naturalized only recently.

LOU: Recently? Well, it took a long time, but anyway at least you are. Dr. Mehdi, what would you have thought of the Israelis had they decided to go to war against the Arab countries on their Highest Holy day of the year and they started to bomb them and kill them? What would your impression be of them?

MEHDI: What my impression is of them now. They're aggressors, they're aggressors on the High Holy day or otherwise. They're intruders into Palestine, occupied the land of the people and are ready to take more, kill more. They're aggressors.

LOU: I see. In other words, it was alright for them to bomb and go to war on Yom Kippur. You see no problem there. Nothing wrong. But if the Israelis had done it to the Arabs, you would have been in front of the United Nations blasting them as being criminals, murderers and ungodly like people.

MEHDI: Well, they are. That's all.

LOU: Oh, of course. You know the Bible, like the Rabbi says. Let me ask you something else. You're pro-Jesse Jackson. Let me ask you one question regarding Jesse Jackson other than the fact that he's pro-Arab, anti-American, anti-white, anti-everything except Arabs. And I don't understand that part either because you know something? We didn't go in and get him out of in chains. You people did.

You brought his people out of Africa with chains. But tell me something—

(NOTE: Here again, Lou tries to smear the Arabs as if by doing so he will justify Jewish occupation of Palestine. And, of course, the author is not responsible for the wrong deeds that the Arabs did, any more than Kahane is responsible for the wrong deeds of the Jews in the past or Bob Grant is responsible for the wrong deeds of the Christians. But logic has no place in the thinking of the Zionists in their attempt to justify their action against the Palestinians.)

MEHDI: Wait, wait. Let me answer you to what you said. In the first place, Jesse Jackson is not pro-Arab. He's not anti-American. He's against racism. He is—

LOU: But . . . but—

MEHDI: Wait, wait, wait, wait. He's against racism in South Africa, in Palestine, in America—

GRANT: Hey, wait a minute. This is the Bob Grant show. I'm not gonna just sit here and allow you to say something that's so patently untrue, such an egregious falsehood. Jesse Jackson is, himself, one of the *prima facie* racists on the face of the earth today. He is perhaps the number one racist in America today. Every word out of his mouth is racist. So don't tell me he's against racism.

MEHDI: In your opinion, Bob, he is because you support the racist governments in South Africa—

GRANT: Oh, that's absurd. That's absurd.

MEHDI: —in Palestine, the Israelis. At any rate, in his—

GRANT: Wait a minute. The Israelis?

MEHDI: Are the racists of all times. To say that they have the right to occupy Palestine because three thousand years ago some Jews had occupied that land. What more deep racism is there?

KAHANE: That's racism?

MEHDI: They segregate, discriminate against the Arab population. And the Rabbi, my own—Rabbi sitting here says that in his Israel, there will be no Arabs. To have a pure Jewish state.

GRANT: Wait a minute, wait a minute. Let's not dwell exclusively on Meir Kahane's quite frank, candid acceptance of the demographic realities of life. Let's talk about the demographic realities all over the world. Maybe this type of voting with one's feet, maybe this type of moving around isn't such a bad idea. And it's not all that new. It's not all that radical. History has shown there've been many times

114

when people have moved. Now maybe that's what we oughta start thinking on a global basis.

(NOTE: Again, the pro-Zionist moderator interferes, defending his fellow Zionist, Kahane. And, indeed, Kahane's theory that because of the demographic realities the Arab population will increase, a solution may be found by kicking out the Arabs or having them vote with their feet.)

MEHDI: Bob, that is a very good, constructive suggestion and I suggest that I have no reservation if the five, six million American Jews go to Israel. The Soviet Jews to go there. They may get a taste of the Jewish ghetto and then vote with their feet, get out of the hole—it will be peaceful. It will be in the interest of the experiment. And if it—peacefully they want to stay there, it will be in the interest of peace.

KAHANE: Listen, Dr. Mehdi, that is really a great, great concept. Why don't we start with the Syrian Jews? Why don't you tell Assad to let the five thousand Jews of Syria vote with their feet, visit Israel and then they'll see how terrible it was, it is in Israel and how wonderful it really was in Syria? Give them a chance. Are you ready to have Assad right at this minute, to get up and say, "Assad, let the Syrian Jews go."

MEHDI: Rabbi, I address at the moment the Syrian Mission to the United Nations, the Ambassador of the Syrian Mission. Please. I shall write tomorrow to President Assad, asking him to let all the Syrian Jews who want to leave to go.

KAHANE: Wonderful.

GRANT: Great.

MEHDI: And then, like the Jews of Iraq who are in Israel and are trying to run out, some of them to return to Baghdad, most of them to come to America—

KAHANE: Some of them want to go back to Baghdad?

MEHDI: Correct. Because—

KAHANE: That snake pit? What are you talking about?

MEHDI: Wait, wait, don't, don't—

GRANT: You have evidence that these Jews who have gone to Israel, some of them want to return to Baghdad, Iraq?

MEHDI: I meet with—

GRANT: You have evidence of that?

MEHDI: I meet with them in Brooklyn. I meet with them in Queens.

KAHANE: You meet with them in Brooklyn and Queens?

MEHDI: Because they couldn't—

KAHANE: And that's Israel?

MEHDI: Exactly. There are—

GRANT: And they want to go to Baghdad?

MEHDI: It is true.

KAHANE: Give me five names and I will print those names in bold letters in the Jewish press. Just five names.

LOU: The tooth fairy is one of them.

MEHDI: Oh, very good. You are very funny, but there are. In New York City alone, we have about half a million Israeli Jews who've run out—

GRANT: Dr. Mehdi, you never cease to amaze me.

MEHDI: Bob, in New York City, we have half a million former Israelis.

GRANT: I know we have a half million Israelis. They're all driving cabs like maniacs—

MEHDI: Exactly.

GRANT: —like maniacs up Sixth Avenue.

MEHDI: Many of them are Iraqi Jews. Many of them are Syrian Jews.

GRANT: Do Iraqi Jews drive cabs?

KAHANE: They certainly don't want to go back to Iraq.

MEHDI: Certainly they don't want to go back to Israel either. But some of them, believe me, want to go back to Baghdad.

KAHANE: They want to go back to Iraq?

MEHDI: Of course.

GRANT: (SINGS) I gotta go back to my little shack in. . .

KAHANE: Not even the Iraqis want to live in Iraq.

MEHDI: Rabbi, please listen. Because the Jews in Iraq were the top of the society—

KAHANE: If the U.S. government opened up its quota system, there would be nobody left in Baghdad.

GRANT: Can you believe this? He said—you've gotta produce these people. I'll put them on the Bob Grant show.

MEHDI: Okay.

LOU: Can I get my nickel's worth in here?

MEHDI: Go ahead, go ahead.

LOU: I have another question for you. I have two questions. I'll make them quick. How much money does Mr. Qaddafi send to Mr. Jackson, Jesse Jackson, the Reverend Jesse Jackson? And don't deny that he doesn't send the money.

116

MEHDI: I really don't know.

LOU: You don't know. Well, you don't know—

GRANT: Well, he doesn't send him the money direct. I think first it goes to Farakhan, and then it goes to—

(NOTE: Grant, the moderator, has no evidence whatsoever, that there is any fund going from Qaddafi to Jackson through Farakhan. However, he has to pour dirt on all the people. And pouring dirt and filth with their mouths is an attribute of some moderators.)

LOU: That may very well be, but he gets it. One more question, if you don't mind. Being president of the United States is the highest position in the world, as far as we're concerned. Can you give me one qualification or one reason you want Jesse Jackson, one qualification he has to be the president of the greatest country in the world?

MEHDI: He's a U.S. born. That is the first.

LOU: You're not answering—

MEHDI: No, I'm—you asked me one qualification. I said he is U.S. born. If you don't know your Constitution, article two, paragraph six, that is your problem.

GRANT: He meant a qualification above and beyond—

MEHDI: The legal—well, the man has an international standing. He understands Asia. He understands Africa. He understands Latin America. And he relates to a large number of the American people, the poor, the deprived, the oppressed. And they are voting for him. That is good enough of a qualification.

LOU: Doctor, thirteen percent.

MEHDI: Well, at the moment is good enough if he later proves that he appeals to greater number and he makes it, then he becomes the qualified person.

GRANT: Lou, Jackson represents the quintessential fox guarding the chicken coop because he would preside over the dismantling of the United States of America, as we have known it. It would become vestigal to the Third World and the Soviet block. It would be an absolute—it would be a travesty that would stagger the imagination. Lou, I thank you for the call.

LOU: One thing. Rabbi?

KAHANE: Yes, sir.

LOU: Get on with that Jews Against Jackson. It's a disgrace the way some of them back him.

KAHANE: You're telling me. You're telling me.

GRANT: Alright. Let's say hello now to Betty here on WABC. You know, in your—I would bet, M.T. Mehdi, that way down deep, way, way deep inside, you really are not for Jesse Jackson. Go ahead, Betty.

BETTY: Yeah, I'd like to ask this of Mr. Mehdi. Israel is the only country in the world that declared itself Jewish. There is no other land that will say, "I am Jewish. Let my brothers come here." Only Israel. Israel is surrounded by over ten, or I don't know how many Arab countries, ten. And they're rich countries. They export oil. I mean, you have people living there. I don't know how rich or what. Can anyone of them find a little piece of land for their own brothers, their own Moslem brothers and take them in? I mean, Israel took in the Ethiopians. They'll take anybody and their own little piece of land because they're their brother, regardless of their color or what they look like. Can't any Arab country take their own brothers? Four thousand, are they such a big problem?

(NOTE: Betty is either innocent or naive. The Jews are trying to bring other Jews to the home of the Palestinians, which they have captured. This, Betty doesn't know or doesn't understand. And whether this is a "little piece of land" or a large piece of land, it is a little piece of the land of the Palestinians, not a little piece of land of the Russians or the Poles or the Americans. It is so easy to be generous to the poor Jews at the expense of the poor Palestinians.)

MEHDI: Betty, you are raising a good question, but with wrong assumptions. And the original assumptions. It is not a question of land. It is a question of recognizing that the Palestinians want to go back to Palestine just as, at least, the Jews of Brooklyn and Los Angeles, after three thousand years, claim that they have the right to Palestine. If the Jews of Poland, Nigeria, Ethiopia—

BETTY: The Jews were thrown out of Poland. They're not wanted in Poland. They were thrown out of Austria and Germany—

MEHDI: Betty, Palestinians were—

BETTY: If the Arabs were thrown out of Israel, look how many Arab countries could find one nice place, build them some housing. Look at the housing the Israelis built for the Ethiopians. Four thousand people are such a problem?

MEHDI: Betty, the Palestinians were also thrown out of their land. And if it is bad for the Jews to be thrown out of Poland, and it is, it is equally bad for the Palestinians to be thrown out of their Palestine. And please listen to me. I plead with you. If the Jews, after three thousand years, haven't forgotten Palestine, the Jews of Brooklyn

118

and Bronx, for heaven's sake, don't expect the Palestinians to forget about Palestine after forty years.

KAHANE: Dr. Mehdi—

BETTY: But there is a place for them to go. There is another Moslem country. There is no other Jewish country.

MEHDI: Why not New York, New York? We'll make New York a Jewish state, a separate, sovereign Jewish state.

KAHANE: You have no right to do that in New York. It belongs—

MEHDI: We have the right—because you don't like the Jews, because—

KAHANE: It belongs to America. It belongs to America, what are you talking about?

MEHDI: Well, Palestine belongs to the Palestinians.

KAHANE: Who are you to come from Baghdad and tell people here, "Make New York State something Jewish?" It is not a—it is not Jewish. It is American.

MEHDI: We should make it a Jewish state.

KAHANE: We should not do that!

MEHDI: Why not? You don't like the Jews here?

KAHANE: You have no right! You have no rights to any part of this country as a Jewish state.

MEHDI: Likewise, Jews have no right to Palestine. That's it.

KAHANE: There is no Palestine. The name Palestine is not an Arabic name. It's a Roman name.

MEHDI: Whatever. What does that mean—?

KAHANE: What does it mean? It means that the Romans conquered the land of Israel. They changed it to Palestine and suddenly we have Palestinians. Had they originally quoted Disneyland, what would we have today?

MEHDI: They would call themselves the people of Disneyland.

(NOTE: Kahane flatly says that, "There is no Palestine." Why? Because "Palestine is not an Arabic name. It is a Roman name." So what?

Theodore Herzel wrote a book to establish a Jewish state in Palestine. The Balfour Declaration promised a national home for the Jews in Palestine. Chaim Wiseman traveled to Palestine. So did Menachim Begin and David Ben-Gurion and Aba Eban and the rest of the Zionists.

The United Nations, in 1947, partitioned Palestine. The Palestinians have an organization called the Palestine Liberation Organization, et cetera, et cetera. Yet in broad daylight and on national airwaves,

Rabbi Kahane states publicly that there is no Palestine because of the absurd logic that "It is a Roman name." How can you argue with persons of this logic and this mentality?)

KAHANE: That's right. That's exactly—

MEHDI: The important thing is that people identify themselves as they wish and you should respect that. Otherwise, this is another racist remark of yours.

KAHANE: Sir, you had an opportunity for a Palestine in 1947. It was the Palestinians that turned it down. You gambled and you lost. And when you lose, you lose.

(NOTE: Again, when Kahane is confronted with facts and the absurdity of his logic, he changes the subject and talks about 1947 and the fact that the disorganized Arabs lost the war against the organized international Zionist movement, which had the backing of the two major powers on earth.)

GRANT: Let's say hello to Abe here very quickly on WABC. Yes Abe. Are you there?

ABE: Hello, Bob?

GRANT: Yes, Abe.

ABE: Okay. I would like to ask—I'm not pro-Israel or pro-Arab. I would like to ask this question anyway to Dr. Mehdi. I, as a black American, I would like to ask this question. You are saying that Jesse Jackson is for the best interest of the poor people of blacks. I would like to ask this. Since Jesse Jackson is the best friend of Farrakhan and Farrakhan is the best friend of Mr. Quadaffi of Libya, now I would like to ask you this. And please do not interrupt me. First of all, everybody knows that Quadaffi, until this very day, he is murdering his own people day in and day out (SOUND OF CLICK)

GRANT: Abe? I guess we lost Abe. Abe? I guess we lost him. Alright, we're going to—we lost Abe. I have no idea what happened to him. Maybe Farrakhan snuck up behind—who knows?

(TRAFFIC REPORT)

GRANT: On WBAC, let's try to squeeze in a couple of more telephone calls for our friendly adversaries. Mario, hello.

MARIO: Hello, Bob.

GRANT: Yes.

MARIO: I'd like to ask Mr. Mehdi—

MEHDI: Yes, Mario.

MARIO: If I'm pronouncing it correctly.

MEHDI: You are. Congratulations.

MARIO: Why do you refuse to direct yourself to the fact that Arabs cannot live in peace with anybody, never mind Jews or Christians. They can't live in peace with themselves. And why don't you address yourself to the fact that Arabs were the first ones to go into Central Africa and hunt blacks and bring them into Egypt and other parts of Arabia as slaves to work for them like beasts of burden. And how can you ally yourself with Jesse Jackson, who's one of the great-grandchildren of one of the slaves that your ancestors probably captured and brought here?

(NOTE: Here again, Mario introduces the irrelevant. Why shouldn't the author support Jackson, whether his great grandfather was a slave or not, and whether the author's ancestors had captured slaves or not? What has all that to do with the author's right to support a presidential candidate? And what has all this to do with the right of the Jews of France or the Bronx to go and occupy Palestine?

It may be difficult for the rest of us to see the relationship between the author and Reverend Jackson through their great grandfathers. But the "collectivist" Zionist mentality, which links a modern Jew from Manhattan, New York who appreciates David Hume, Bach and supports the 19th Amendment to the U.S. Constitution—If the Zionist mind can relate this modern Jew to those primitive Hebrew tribes who burnt down Jericho in the name of God,—the same Zionist collectivist mind can relate the author to Jackson and be astonished at the author's support of Reverend Jackson's candidacy for President! Is that collectivist mind of the Zionists a sick mind? Or is it only absurd!)

MEHDI: Mario, your first question, that the Arabs cannot live in peace with each other, is not correct. There are Arab conflicts, but that is possibly the exception than the rule. Now you may be asking why aren't there Jewish conflicts in Israel? Well, the Jews are not killing Jews today thanks to the Arabs. The moment there is peace, then you'll find Jews killing Jews in Israel by thousands.

KAHANE: That's nonsense. That is nonsense.

MEHDI: The Jews should be grateful to the Arabs because they are not killing each other.

KAHANE: That is nonsense.

MARIO: Who do you think you're talking to? You're talking to pretty intelligent people in this country. You're not talking to Arabs.

MEHDI: No, I'm talking to you and if you are intelligent, so you raise your question, then you listen.

MARIO: We're not idiots here.

MEHDI: Some of you are.

MARIO: We are educated in this country.

MEHDI: Some of you are. Some of you are not. I don't know in which category you are. But you ask about the question of Arabs engaging in slavery. That is, to the extent that it is true, those Arabs were SOB's. I denounce the Arabs who engaged in it. The Jews provided the money and those Jews were—

KAHANE: What Jews provided the money? What are—?

MEHDI: —SOB's. And the Christians purchased them and those Christians—

KAHANE: What are you talking about? What Jews provided the money? Wait, wait, wait! Wait, wait! What—

MEHDI: —and those Christians were SOB's.

KAHANE: —Jews provided the money? What Jews provided the money? Where? Where? Where?

MEHDI: Same time that the supposedly Arabs engaged in the capturing—

KAHANE: Supposedly the Arabs did?

MEHDI: The Jews provided the money and the Christians purchased the slaves.

KAHANE: What Jews?

MARIO: I want you to prove—

MEHDI: And those Arabs were SOB's and those Jews were SOB's. And those Christians were SOB's.

KAHANE: Doctor Mehdi. You're a loser today.

GRANT: You know, the real M.T. Mehdi is coming out now. The real M.T. Mehdi is coming out.

MEHDI: I'm denouncing all the evil-doers—

GRANT: What a slanderous statement. He asked you what Jews were providing the money. You can't even tell him.

MEHDI: Well, he cannot give me which Arabs were capturing the slaves.

KAHANE: But everyone knows and history knows that—

MEHDI: Rabbi, you—not everybody. You know.

KAHANE: —the slave trade was an Arab slave trade. And, indeed, the U.N. has stated that there is still black slavery today in Arabia. Today.

MEHDI: If it is, I denounce it. I am responsible for my own deeds. Those Arabs who do such—

KAHANE: But you are the only righteous Arab left in Sodom.

MARIO: But the rest are all Soddomites, sir.

MEHDI: Rabbi, you are being discourteous again and I forgive you again. The point really—

KAHANE: But Dr. Mehdi, but I don't lie.

MEHDI: —is that we should be courageous to denounce all the evil doers, whether they're Arabs—

(NOTE: For the role of "some" Jews in slavery, see Encyclopaedia Judaica, *Vol. 14, Macmillan, published in Israel, 1971, P. 1660:*

"Slave Trade. *Jews engaged in slave trade—although they never played a prominent role in it—from the early Middle Ages to early modern period."*

Slaves ". . .were of the few 'commodities' that Europe could export to the Byzantine and later Muslim Mediterrenean, from which it imported so much, thus restoring the balance of payments. The Jewish slave owner, however, was expected by the Church to release his slave the moment the latter converted to Christianity. Jews also used slaves in their vineyards."

"Emperor Louis I the Pious granted a number of Jews (c. 825-8) the right to import foreign slaves and sell them within the confines of the Empire."

"In the Americas *until 1730 the Dutch West Indies Company maintained a monopoly on the importation of slaves into all the Dutch colonies in the Americas, but Jews appear to have been among the major retailers of slaves in Dutch Brazil (1630-54), because Jews possessed ready money and were willing to trade slaves for sugar." Etc. Etc. till page 1664.*

GRANT: Let's try and take another call. Ben, you're on WABC. Go ahead please.

BEN: Hello, Dr. Mehdi.

MEHDI: Yes, sir.

BEN: I'd like to ask you a question. Could you, in all God's truth, say—speculate as to what would have happened to the Jewish population in Israel or Palestine, whatever you want to call it, what would have happened if any of the—if the Arabs had won any of the wars? Especially the first one.

MEHDI: Ben, you remember I've said earlier that eight hundred years ago today—

BEN: Never mind eight hundred years ago. Now?

MEHDI: Wait. Eight hundred—wait, please.

BEN: Don't give me a monologue.

MEHDI: Wait, please, wait one second. Wait one second. Eight hundred years ago today the Arab Muslims entered Jerusalem, liberating it. They respected the conquered, the vanquished Europeans. They honored them. And the same will happen when the Arabs will liberate Jerusalem again.

GRANT: Alright, Ben. Thank you for the call. Mohammad Mehdi, Meir Kohane. I think we'll have to do this again very soon. Most stimulating. We haven't really solved anything, but then again, did anyone really expect us to?

(NOTE: A personal reflection on Kahane by the author:

As I was sitting next to Kahane for several hours, contemplating his reaction and watching his gestures, I found a pathetic figure of a frightened person. Kahane is the most pessimistic person, full of insecurities and full of fears. You talk about tomorrow and he speaks of yesterday. You express the hope for peace and he talks about the fact that they killed us in 1928 and the Romans expelled us two thousand years ago from Palestine. The man lives in the past, has trouble looking forward to the future. He only sees the bad things in life, with no ability even to hope for better things. The pathetic figure of this frightened person invokes sympathy and pity. He would feel secure only in a purely Jewish ghetto! But then in a completely Jewish ghetto, he would suffocate!

Kahane is the personification of Zionism. Other Zionists are in various degrees similar to Kahane in their fear of the future.

The Jews at large must emancipate themselves psychologically from the pains and horrors of the past in order to eliminate the fear of the future and prepare to live in the prejudice-free world of tomorrow.)

Notes

1. The FBI Report on Terrorism, 1986, Pp. 2–3
2. The New York Times, June 11, 1986, p. A6
3. NYT, August 27, 1986, Pp. 1 and 7
4. The Washington Post, October 2, 1986, p. 1
5. The New York Times, June 11, 1986, p. A13
6. See Menachim Begin, THE REVOLT, The Story of Irgun. Published by Henry Schuman, N. Y. 1951, Pp. 162–165 wherein Begin boasts of the fear and panic created amongst the Palestinians as the result of his attacks on the Arab village of Deir Yassin.
7. For the capture of the Israeli Olympic Village, see *NYT*, Sept. 6, 1972, p. 1. David Berger was buried in Shaker Heights, Ohio. *NYT*, Sept. 9, 1972, p. 4.
8. See Royal Institute of International Affairs, GREAT BRITAIN AND PALESTINE, 1915–1946, London, 1946, Pp. 61–62.
9. The Resolution of the General Syrian Congress of 1919 and recommendations of the King-Crane Commission are quoted in George Antonius, THE ARAB AWAKENING, Hamish Hamilton, London, 1961, Pp. 440–442.
10. For the quotations above see ISRAEL ACCORDING TO THE HOLY SCRIPTURE, published by Igram Press, Cedar Rapids, Iowa, Pp. 15–28, and 45.
11. For the Israeli confiscation of Arab cities, shops and groves see Don Peretz, "Problems of Arab Refugee Compensation," THE MIDDLE EAST JOURNAL, Autumn, 1954, Pp. 403 ff.
12. Roger Baldwin is quoted in William Zukerman's JEWISH NEWS-LETTER, Vol. XV, No. 7, April 1959, p. 4.
13. Erich Fromm is quoted in William Zukerman's JEWISH NEWS-LETTER, May 19, 1958, p. 2.
14. The qualifications of the "American" Col. David Marcus who died fighting for Israel are listed in ISRAEL DIGEST, Published by the Israeli Embassy, Washington, D.C., p. 6.
15. Labouisse's statement is quoted in MIDDLE EAST FORUM, Published by AUB, 1959, p. 24.
16. The views of U.S. Foreign Service men on American policy are to be found in STUDY OF THE UNITED STATES FOREIGN POLICY—Summary of Views of Retired Foreign Service Officers, prepared for the Committee on Foreign Relations, U.S. Senate, pursuant to the provisions of S. Res. 31, 86th Congress, 1st Session, June 15, 1959, Pp. 67–70.
17. According to the FBI, there have been no incidents of terrorism against U.S. citizens by Arabs or Moslems on U.S. soil to date.

Selected Bibliography

Paul Anderson, TERRORISTS OF TOMORROW, 192 Pp., Critics Choice, 1985

Menachim Begin, THE REVOLT: The story of the Irgun, Henry Schuman, New York, 1951

David Ben-Gurion, RE-BIRTH AND DESTINY OF ISRAEL, New York, N.Y. 1954

Ray S. Cline and Yonah Alexander, TERRORISM AS STATE SPONSORED COVERT WARFARE, 128 Pp., Hero Books, 1986

Sheikh Mohammad Hussein Fadlallah, AL-ISLAM WA MANTEQ AL-QUAAT Arabic (ISLAM AND THE LOGIC OF FORCE), Beirut, 3rd ed. 1985

Martha Crenshaw (Ed.), TERRORISM: LEGITIMACY AND POWER: THE CONSEQUENCE OF POLITICAL VIOLENCE by Irving L. Horwitz *et al* 162, Pp., Wesleyan University Press 1986

Timothy B. Garrigan & George A. Lopez, TERRORISM: A PROBLEM OF POLITICAL VIOLENCE, 40 Pp, 1980

Gil Green, TERRORISM: IS IT REVOLUTIONARY?, New Outlook, 1970

Seymur Hersh, "Target Qaddafi" New York Times Magazine, Feb. 22, 1987

Moorhead Kennedy, THE AYATOLLAH IN THE CATHEDRAL, Hill and Wang, New York, 1986

Walter Laqueur, TERRORISM, Little, Brown 1979

M. T. Mehdi, KENNEDY AND SIRHAN...WHY? New World Press, N.Y. 1968

Abraham H. Miller, TERRORISM AND HOSTAGE NEGOTIATIONS, 134 Pp., Westview 1981

———, (Ed.) TERRORISM, THE MEDIA AND THE LAW, 232 Pp., Transnational Publications, 1982

Benjamin Netanyahu (Ed.) TERRORISM: HOW THE WEST CAN WIN, 272 Pp., Avon 1987

Michael J. O'Neill, TERRORISM SPECTACULARS: SHOULD TV COVERAGE BE CURBED?: 109 Pp., Priority, 1986

Bonnie Szumski, TERRORISM: OPPOSING VIEWPOINTS, 200 Pp., Greenhaven, 1986

Edward Tivnan, *The Lobby: Jewish Political Power and American Foreign Policy,* Simon and Schuster, New York, 1987, pp. 304

Ronald Young, *Missed Opportunities,* American Friends Service Committee, Philadelphia, Pa., 1987

Paul Wilkinson, TERRORISM AND THE LIBRAL STATE, 336 Pp., New York University Press, 1986

Robin Wright, SACRED RAGE: THE CRUSADE OF MODERN ISLAM, 315 Pp., Linden Press, 1985